memoir *overcoming
Ac

RAVEN'S MANTLE

RAVEN'S MANTLE

FIGHTING THE BETRAYAL OF AMERICA

RAVEN HARRISON

BROWN BOOKS
PUBLISHING GROUP

Raven's Mantle
Fighting the Betrayal of America

Brown Books Publishing Group
Dallas, TX / New York, NY
www.BrownBooks.com
(972) 381-0009

A New Era in Publishing®

Publisher's Cataloging-In-Publication Data

Names: Harrison, Raven, author.
Title: Raven's mantle : fighting the betrayal of America / Raven Harrison.
Description: Dallas, TX ; New York, NY : Brown Books Publishing Group, [2023]
Identifiers: ISBN: 9781612546247 | LCCN: 2022951684
Subjects: LCSH: Harrison, Raven. | Women conservatives--Texas--Biography.
    | Indian women--Texas-- Biography. | African American women--Texas--
    Biography. | United States--Politics and government--21st century. | LCGFT:
    Autobiographies. | BISAC: BIOGRAPHY & AUTOBIOGRAPHY / Political. |
    BIOGRAPHY & AUTOBIOGRAPHY / Personal Memoirs.
Classification: LCC: JC573.2.U6 H37 2023 | DDC: 320.52092--dc23

ISBN 978-1-61254-624-7
LCCN 2022951684

Printed in the United States
10 9 8 7 6 5 4 3 2 1

For more information or to contact the author, please go to
www.RavenHarrison.com.

Raven's Mantle, whose meaning is both biblical and literal,
is dedicated to God. He is the Bestower and Protector
of my whole heart, life's purpose, and my family.

Patience and Major, your happiness is my life's mission.
I will fight with everything I have to give you the free America
which your grandparents and father fought so bravely for.
I love you beyond words and without measure.

CONTENTS

FOREWORD

I first met Raven Harrison in early 2021 at a DFW Deplorables meeting. I had been the first statewide-elected official in Texas to endorse Donald Trump for president back in 2016 and was a finalist to be his United States Secretary of Agriculture after he won the White House. My strong support for the president had earned me the moniker of "Trump's Man in Texas." It was a title used by the president himself to describe me when he endorsed my reelection campaign in 2018.

I had often referred to myself as a "deplorable" after Hillary Clinton had described all Trump supporters as such in her, now famous, tirade; so I was pleased when I received an invitation to speak at a meeting of my fellow deplorables from the Dallas-Fort Worth Metroplex.

After discussing our mutual admiration for President Trump and our disappointment with the outcome of the 2020 presidential election, I thought I would use the remainder of my allotted time to tell the folks assembled a little bit about some of the lesser-known responsibilities of the Texas Department of Agriculture—the agency I was first elected to lead back in 2014 following a successful twelve-year stint in the Texas House of Representatives.

After providing some insight into the inner workings of the Texas Department of Agriculture (TDA), I asked the crowd one of my favorite questions: "What does the Department of Agriculture have to do with the Texas State Lottery?" It was a question that I had asked to dozens of groups, and no one could ever provide the correct answer . . . until then.

A striking woman whom I had never met before raised her hand and then went on to explain that the TDA was responsible for the regulation of weights and measures and, therefore, was responsible for inspecting the numbered ping-pong balls used each week for lottery drawings to ensure they have not been tampered with and were all uniform in size and weight. I chuckled and said, "You're exactly right," and congratulated her on being the first to ever answer my question correctly. As I took a few last questions, I thought to myself, *That gal has sure done her homework!*

As the meeting came to a close, that same woman came up to me and introduced herself as Raven Harrison and told me she was running for Congress. She thanked me for coming and told me she appreciated my unabashed support of the MAGA movement.

While our introduction was brief, I thought to myself, *This woman is special and is destined for great things.*

I had the opportunity to see Raven from time to time at various GOP events in the metroplex and listen to her speak. I saw Raven as a passionate, articulate, and sincere conservative leader who loved God, loved her family, and loved her country and was willing to fight to protect it for her children and future generations of Americans.

I learned that Raven was the proud daughter of two retired United States Air Force (USAF) officers and that her husband, Paul, was a retired USAF combat pilot. She had grown up learning about sacrifice and the high cost of freedom and how easily it can be lost.

Raven and I have since become close friends. Recently, my wife, Debra, and I joined Raven and Paul on a trip to Washington, DC, for an America First Policy Institute forum with President Trump and count-less conservative leaders from around our country. I got to see Raven in her true element, a natural leader, who is the future of our conservative movement. Countless others saw it too!

During our trip, Raven took us to suburban Maryland to meet her dad. Raven showed Debra and I the trees she climbed as a young girl and the kitchen table where she and her dad discussed the history of our nation, her own Native American heritage, and the important les-sons taught by her ancestors. He and her mom taught her to always be willing to fight for what was right, even if doing so wasn't popular. She has carried those time-honored lessons into her adult life.

Today, my friend is fast becoming one of the most respected conservative voices in America. Whether through her regular appearances on FOX News radio stations across the country, her podcast (*Raven's Radar*), her speaking engagements, her social media outreach that touches millions, or this book (which tells her unique life story in her own words), Raven Harrison has become a Conservative Warrior for all of us who want to be able to hand our children and grandchildren a better America than the one handed to us by our parents and grandparents.

Like me, Raven is someone who says what she means, does what she says, and gets things done. I am proud to call her my friend, and I can't wait to see what she does next.

—Sid Miller,
Commissioner of the Texas Department of Agriculture
and Former Member of the Texas House of Representatives

CHAPTER 1

ACCIDENT

"Freedom is a fragile thing, and it's never more
than one generation away from extinction."
—Ronald Reagan[1]

She screamed through the stoplight, engine redlining as she floored it.
Light metallic paint. It was a Porsche. I knew by the headlights. My
mom had one once.

The accelerating Porsche filled my peripheral view at warp speed. It
was coming right at me.

I hit the brakes. Gripped the wheel.

I thought she'd just miss me, but her SUV swerved. I braced for
impact.

She T-boned me in the intersection, slamming into my driver's side
door. It spun me hard to the right. Radiator fluid flooded my wind-
shield; her SUV crumpled my car like a tin can in a compactor.

I had the best view of the worst movie ever.

Green utility box: missed.

Tree: missed.

Telephone pole: missed.

My car jumped the curb, taking a giant chunk of concrete out of it
as it flew. The cabin filled with the scream of angry, boiling kettles as
airbags deployed around me. In nightmares, I don't feel the shock of
the impact, or the dizzying, out-of-control spinning, or my car coming
to a violent, sideways stop on the sidewalk at the crossing signal. What
makes me wake—shuddering from my nightmares—is the deafening
hiss of the kettles and the burn of their scalding steam enveloping me.

It was Thursday. I was going to the market because we were out of food in the house.

Then *bang!* I was wrapped in a white pillow fortress, and everything went silent for a while.

It was 2022. Winter was ending in North Texas. I had recently lost my primary bid for the United States' House of Representatives for Texas's Twenty-Sixth Congressional District seat in a dirty, corrupt, sewer-esque primary against an almost twenty-year entrenched, career politician. I had expected a contentious fight. I truly did. It was good old boy politics, and I definitely wasn't in the club. I was the only woman, the only native-born Texan, and the only minority on the ballot for District Twenty-Six.

My reception among voters was encouraging and welcoming. They were engaged and asked detailed question. They took great care in getting to know me and what I represented: a native Texan running to represent Texas values. But my reception among the Republican Party leaders was quite different. I was intentionally left off of literature, voting guides, and meet and greets; my signs were removed and destroyed; and many openly gossiped about me at events. I unknowingly walked up behind a county chair during an event telling precinct chairs that I was a "Democrat plant."

I was fighting the betrayal of America, committed by our entrenched leaders, corrupt institutions, milquetoast, in-party traitors, and the liberal media. I'd seen it as an extension of woke, liberal, and career politics driving us to moral decay and sugarcoated socialism. What I didn't expect—and discovered too late—was that even allies inside the Republican Party (some grassroot movements, and trusted leaders—some within my campaign) were saboteurs and part of the fix.

It was a serene white everywhere. My first impression was that I had died.

The immediate reality returned as someone was pulling open my driver door. I couldn't see anyone through the airbags, only feet. People were talking. "It's okay, I have a camera."

"She seems okay."

"We have to get her out to be sure."

My car filled with a white, powdery fog as a firefighter cut the airbags away.

The ambulance was already there, along with a large and growing crowd. It was the first accident I was ever in. After cutting away the still-inflated airbags, the paramedic began to assess my injuries. "Ma'am, where are you hurt? Can you move? You can let go of the steering wheel now."

"My body feels like it's on fire," I mumbled. Like someone pouring acid on my face and neck, burning through my clothes.

They examined me briefly, decided my injuries needed immediate medical attention, and carefully extracted me from the car. The more I moved, the more it hurt. The elation I felt surviving the crash and standing on my own two feet was replaced by pain when my right leg buckled.

There was a woman sitting on the green utility box. Paramedics were assessing her, and she glared at me.

"Did she get caught in the accident?" I asked, limping toward the ambulance, supported by two firefighters. My right leg was bent at the wrong angle, and I couldn't walk on my own.

The firefighters exchanged glances, and the bigger of the two shook his head. "That's the woman who hit you."

She locked eyes with me as I went by and shouted, "I know who you are."

Once I was clear of the debris, they strapped me to a gurney.

Her car was smoldering, and her engine was puddling fluids on the road.

"My body," shouted the woman. "My choice."

"If it was your body, it would be you who dies." It was surreal. "You could have killed me. My body doesn't want to be killed! That's my choice."

They eased my gurney into the ambulance. My heart was racing because of the size of the crowd that had gathered. Policemen were directing traffic around the accident.

During my campaign, there were attempts to attack and malign me. I wondered what pictures of me, looking like this, would be on the news or on billboards the next morning. It would be out of context and whatever was most humiliating. That was their game.

I was driving my husband's, Paul, car when the accident occurred. My SUV was still in the shop after getting caught in the Kalahari tornado. My husband loves gadgets and technology, and this car, a royal blue Tesla, was his favorite—we named it Subzero. He was meticulous and kept it mint. I had a good view of what was left of Subzero from the ambulance while they put in my IV. It was royally dead.

The day would have been a picturesque, sunny, almost-springtime afternoon . . . if she hadn't had hit me, destroying Paul's car, and the EMTs weren't cutting my jeans to tatters to examine my legs. One leg was obviously broken. My ankles were purple and swollen. The pain was unbelievable.

In addition to being shaken to the core, I was also terrified of the discussions taking place among the emergency personnel on the scene. I held the ambulance door open with my nonbroken leg, and I frantically waved for a patrolman to come over while I could still talk. After all I had experienced during the campaign—the backdoor deals, the bogus smear tactics, and unholy alliances that had rallied against me—there was no way I was leaving until I gave my account of the accident. I'd seen how readily and easily my political opponents distorted the truth. I trusted no one. The police needed all the facts, before the story broke and the spinning began.

"Ma'am, we need to get you to a hospital right away."

"I'm not leaving until I tell my side of it!" I was bruised and bleeding, but unwavering.

"Okay, ma'am, what happened?"

I went through the particulars fast. "She hit me. I had the right-of-way."

"Thanks, ma'am. We got that on a dashcam recording of the accident. You're hurt pretty bad, and the EMTs need to take you to the hospital now. We'll update your husband and let him know where they're taking you."

The driver was still hollering, "I know who you are."

I was terrified to be the first to leave the accident scene. One of the paramedics had retrieved my phone and handed it to me. Paul was calling. The Tesla had a safety featured that notified Paul via the app on his phone and then automatically called my number. Tesla technology is second to none, but I still preferred my big, heavy SUV. You just can't take the Texas out of me.

I was desperate to explain that I wasn't distracted or careless. "It wasn't my fault!" I screamed through a flood of tears.

"I know, darling, and it doesn't matter. Thank God you are alright. Let them take you to the hospital. The kids and I will meet you there. Everything is going to be alright. I love you." I withdrew my swollen-leg barrier, and they closed the ambulance doors.

She could have killed me. *Was this an accident? Or was she so consumed with hate that she was willing to take my life?*

The police investigated whether the accident was intentional; but except for her speeding up as she swerved into me, screaming "my body, my choice," and claiming that she knew who I was, there wasn't enough evidence to proceed.

Paul and the kids met me at the hospital.

I reiterated, "It wasn't my fault," but he didn't care about the car, only that I was alright—that's one of the many reasons I love him. I used to joke that I would be toast if I ever got into an accident in his "stupid space car." I have to admit, the Tesla saved my life. The exterior was destroyed, but I was immediately walled into a pillow fortress. Paul had researched the safety features ad nauseam, and thank God he did.

My daughter, Patience, stopped cold in her tracks when she saw me. Her big brown eyes sparkled wet and gold, about to cry.

I imagine I looked like I was in a bad bar fight: black eye, bandages, and my nearly broken back in a brace. Second-degree burns covered my hands from the airbag deployment. I did what mothers often do: I sucked up the unconscionable pain, put on a brave smile, and reassured her that, despite the optics, her mom would live to see another day. "It's okay, baby, Mommy's fine. You should see the other guy." I smiled. It wasn't pretty, but the warrior in me would not allow my children to be frightened by it, so I smiled through the pain.

Her terrified look turned to gushing pride, as if her mom had just slayed a mighty dragon.

My youngest, Major, was scared until he saw my crutches and got to try them out. He began doing a time-honored tradition of long-distance crutch jumping to pass the time in the hospital. Crutches were new for him, and he was an instant pro, swinging and leaping and racing around the room, wondering why anyone would not want crutches.

When they cleared me to leave the hospital, Paul went to bring the car around.

I asked for a wheelchair, both for the pain and for discretion. Of course, they were all out. It was that kind of day, but I was ready to go. The emergency room was now full of people, and I despised being a spectacle. In a wheelchair, no one would have noticed my now-shredded,

Bruce Banner-looking jeans. But on crutches, I felt I would be the main attraction.

I tried to have a sense of humor, joking that the least they could do for me—looking like I did with my pants cut to the thighs and in tatters; every part of me swollen; my body bruised yellow, green, and purple—was play the theme from *The Incredible Hulk*.

The doctor rubbed his stubble, thought about it, and said, "I could make that happen."

And he did. With the magic of YouTube, he played the theme from *The Incredible Hulk* over the intercom as I crutched and pretended to hitchhike my way out of the hospital.

It was epic, and it included the "You wouldn't like me when I'm angry" voice-over.

Most of the waiting room were people over a certain age who instantly got it when they saw me shambling through the lobby, like I'd just Hulk'd out. The lobby erupted into a thunderous applause, clapping and cheering as I made my way to the car with my kids flanked on either side of me. I got a standing ovation and confirmation that people had great taste in classic TV.

My kids didn't get it at all, but they were happy that I was happy. Teenagers rolled their eyes, and Paul, who'd gone all the way to the shop to get my SUV, was confused when he opened the door for me. "Uh . . . Raven? Why are people applauding you leaving the hospital?"

I told him on the way home.

With the help of a few people, I ended a terrible, painful day with a moment that put smiles on a lot of faces. It's still a pleasant memory, and proof that you never really know what can happen until you try.

I went home to Frisco with my leg propped up. Patience leaned against the couch with her head on my stomach, telling me a story while I stroked her luxurious halo of knee-length hair. Her locks have earned her the obvious nickname "Rapunzel," which stuck once she started doing commercials for Disney. Then Major wandered in hungry, and Patience led him away to hunt for snacks. She was my Florence Nightingale, ensuring no further harm would come to me on her watch.

I could hear her chiding Major downstairs for pole vaulting with my crutches.

Paul is a towering six-foot-seven, retired Air Force aviator we have nicknamed "Mach Daddy." He's now a commercial management, technical pilot for the airlines. He's tall, dark-haired, and handsome with golden-brown eyes the same color as Patience's. I'd say he's the strong, silent type. Paul might acknowledge that he's stoic, but he attends to our family with the same caring precision as the aircrafts he flies, like he's following some checklist that covers every potential need and contingency. We feel it and benefit from his care and attention every single day. It would annoy me if it wasn't so damn endearing.

I feel blessed and spoiled by his love.

Scars remain on my neck and hands, the bruises have faded, my fractured leg is healing, and I'm enduring months of physical therapy so I can walk again—hopefully without a limp.

Recovery gave me time to think and reflect.

The recovery was hard and continues to this day. My invisible scars have taken longer to heal, but I'm surrounded by people I love.

Did the first round of my fight for public office and recent accident discourage me?

Not even a little. Life is unique in that you get the test before the lesson. It was twelve years from the time the prophet Samuel anointed David before he became king. My goals are not that lofty, but the lesson is the same: God works on His schedule, not mine. Surviving this accident is testament to God's faithful protection of those who seek Him. The call, the campaign, and everything that led to the accident has reinforced what is truly important, and listening to my kids rustling through the kitchen talking about their futures and what they aspire to be only steels my resolve: America is built on an ideal, that all men are created equal and endowed by our Creator with inalienable rights to Life, Liberty, and the Pursuit of Happiness. We need God back—now more than ever.

No other nation on Earth believed in those inalienable rights. Not until the Declaration of Independence asserted those truths and our people fought for those rights in the Revolutionary War.

Abraham Lincoln called the Declaration of Independence "a rebuke and a stumbling-block to tyranny and oppression."[2] During the American Civil War, he said in the Gettysburg Address, "that we here highly resolve these dead shall not have died in vain; that the nation, shall have a new birth of freedom, and that government of the people by the people for the people, shall not perish from the earth."[3] Going into the war, it was widely believed that he would fail, becoming the last president of the United States. But President Lincoln succeeded, and after the Civil War, he abolished slavery and reunited our nation.

One hundred thousand union soldiers gave their lives to free slaves they never owned. People question me, as a minority woman, if I am on the right side of history. I like to remind them that I am, figuratively and literally. Lest we forget, Abraham Lincoln led this country through war, abolished slavery, and healed a land divided.

Historically illiterate, woke protestors who tear down his statues, labeling him an oppressor and racist are not well versed in history. I am still surprised at the number of protestors that think they can change history by erasing it. The politicians running those cities, who swore an oath to protect and defend the Constitution, shouldn't tolerate it. We should question why they do. The dark chapters in our shared history are not to be altered or erased, but rather learned from to ensure they are never repeated.

It's important to revisit where it all began, to remember where we come from, to celebrate how far we've come, and to understand the dream so each generation can uphold its authenticity and keep it alive.

I want that freedom without fear or apology for my children, my family, and every citizen of this great country. Even though our leaders, our institutions, and the media have betrayed America, we are resilient. We will get it back.

One thing history and life have taught me is that if you don't fight for what you believe in, you'll lose it. Those countries that have lost freedom have yet to restore it. I believe in America. For over 245 years, the United States has been proving everyone wrong and leading change and innovation across the world. The good parts of who we are as people and a nation can always overcome the bad.

I was a military brat long before I built my first business. Now I'm a wife, mother, and warrior on the front lines fighting for the America I once knew.

My mother was a US Air Force officer, raising me almost by herself in the 1970s. She was a petite yet powerful lady. She never missed one Sunday of church. She would give you her last dollar, but she would also tear you to shreds if you trifled with her. My mother graduated from the University of Houston with a degree in electrical electronics engineering. She was the only woman and only minority in the program. Professors refused to grade her assignments, and the university dean would have to intervene.

She was blazing a trail in the military that future generations of women would follow. To do that, she had to perform her duties better than anyone else and go anywhere they needed her skills. Every day she was running a gauntlet. Any misstep would add fuel to the fire that she didn't belong in this man's air force.

I don't know exactly what she did because much of her work was classified. Later, I learned she was involved in engineering and program management, but even to this day, details remain cloaked in a veil of secrecy. I heard the term "satellite defense systems" a lot, but no idea where she fit into it. What she impressed upon me was that discipline, self-sufficiency, and an education were my keys to a better life. As a child, I could see how hard she worked. It was a time when women were integrating into a predominately male, military-combat force, and that change was neither easy nor welcome.

My journey was similar. I didn't fit in. I'm a mix of Native American, African, Anglo American, and Irish. I just considered myself American, but schools and society needed to label me. They needed me to fit into a neat category.

If I had a dollar for every time I've been asked "What are you?", I could make a real dent in world hunger. I was too dark to be white, and too light to be black.

I was extremely intelligent, but I had to learn not to be too smart, as being smart wasn't always an asset. It added a layer of jealousy to the bigotry and hate.

My mom was a Temporary Duty Assignment (TDA) and went on a lot of missions doing things in places she couldn't talk about. Trying to fill her in on my life while she was gone and hearing her say "uh-huh" or "that's nice" until she was snoring, sound asleep in her uniform while I covered her with a blanket, was the norm. I think I tucked her in more than she tucked me in.

There was never a time Mom did just one thing—ever. She was always multitasking five things at once. If she was on the phone, she was also washing dishes and reviewing my homework. If she was driving, she was also dictating notes or practicing her lector duties for church. I remember my mother taking me and a friend to Bush Gardens when laptop computers were new technology and still big, and awkward to lug around. She brought her computer to the park and the only place she could plug it in was the gift shop.

So there she was, sitting in the middle of Bush Gardens—amidst the roller coasters, fountains, and concession stands—typing away while my friend and I and the park guests lived it up. The extension cord to her laptop was so long and out of place at the amusement park that the staff reported it to security as a safety hazard. They couldn't wrap their heads around it, asking why she wouldn't just stay home and work if she was that busy.

She simply replied, "I can't disappoint my daughter."

My days were long, hard, and physically exhausting. I was at the bus stop for school at 6:00 a.m. and wouldn't get picked up until 7:00 p.m. She packed my lunch to include my breakfast, lunch, and dinner. My legs and back hurt constantly from the weight of carrying three meals every day, but Mom never took a day off, so neither could I. I loved my mom, I was proud of her, and I worked hard to be a good girl.

I felt a sense of guilt that was sometimes overwhelming. Her life was unduly hard because she had me. She had way too much on her plate working long hours, sometimes here, but often away.

Children pick up on the emotions, stress, and discord around them and often feel responsible for it, or at fault, and I was no different. So I left behind sports, friends, and extracurricular activities to avoid adding to her burden. This was during the Cold War. She was busy keeping us safe from communist Russia, North Korea, and China, and I didn't want to be trouble. I wanted her to be proud of me, and I worked hard too. It would kill me to disappoint her. So I became a top student, I learned to be reliable, and I didn't complain, even when I should have.

I looked up to her. We had each other's six, even when she was gone, and I missed her. No matter where her duties took her, no matter how hard things got, I knew everything would be fine because she was my mom and my hero. She still is.

I stayed with a lot of families while Mom was away. It was a common thing in the military. Air force families looked after each other, and wives always wanted to babysit because it was a great way to earn extra money without disrupting their family life in on-base housing. So I had quite a few sitters, and I tried to be the perfect kid because I didn't want my mother ever hearing I misbehaved. It wasn't that I was afraid of her. She worked so hard; I just couldn't do it to her.

When we were first stationed at Ramstein Air Base in Germany, some wives acted like moms when I stayed with them, and their families treated me like I was part of their family. I became friends with their kids and tried to stay with them when Mom was away, but military families always move on, and the best sitters always seemed to leave the fastest for their next assignment.

The military families that never seemed to leave were always a little different, and some wives were straight up crazy. One was a German lady, Hilda, who was married to an American serviceman. She used to blow smoke rings into my face.

The worst of them I'll never forget. Her name was Dolly. Dolly was a tall, porky, dark-haired woman with four kids who were goobers. People considered her a no-nonsense woman whose children were seemingly well-behaved to the point of absolute, machine-like compliance. She was imposing from a child's perspective: her rule was law, and her kids learned early that disobedience had severe physical consequences. She was sweet as pecan pie around my mother, only to go full Jekyll-and-Hyde the second Mom was gone.

When my mom left for a three-week deployment to a place called Ascension Island, it followed busy weeks when she was at work zero dark thirty and home late at night. We didn't talk. She left me notes full of things I needed to remember to do. The first thing she said to me in weeks was, "Be good. I love you. Goodbye."

She handed Dolly a manila envelope full of the cash they'd agreed on for food, and for expenses to watch me. My mother's Ascension Island secure contact information was written neatly on it in black ballpoint pen. For all I knew, Ascension Island was the Island of Lost Toys or Neverland.

She left on a Tuesday. That night, Dolly made a special steak dinner. We gathered around the table. She set the steaks down with a flourish, and they were bleeding.

Dolly called it rare, but none of the slabs of meat looked look like they'd even touched the grill. I tried my best to avoid the gross yellow fat and eat around the paler edges of the raw beef as much as I could, but the flavor was awful. My mouth filled with the taste of iron blood, and it sickened me. I looked up. She was watching me.

"May I please have mine cooked a bit more?" I asked, and without warning, she exploded.

"We don't waste food in this house! I don't know what kinda posh lifestyle you're used to, but here, when we have meat, it's eaten as given." She was cruel, threatened violence, and didn't hold back because I was a child.

I didn't know where to look or what to do, so I took it. I tried to swallow the raw, red meat I hacked off the steak, but I couldn't. I gagged on it. Then, the meat was back on my plate again.

The other kids wolfed down dinner, got up, and left to play.

I stood. Dolly yelled, "Don't you dare leave until you clean your plate!"

I tried to eat. The best I could do was not throw up.

It was 6:00 p.m. I resolved to not cry. I sat there three-and-a-half more hours. At 9:30 p.m., she turned on the kitchen light. "Now you can get up."

I brushed my teeth longer and better than I ever had in my life. Cindy, the daughter three years younger than me, was already asleep in the bottom bunk. And I climbed into bed thinking, *Why am I even here? It's not fair.* I wondered what Mom was doing. If she had even reached that island, somewhere, so she could do something she couldn't tell me about.

I sighed, my stomach growled, and I moaned into my pillow. Of course, there was lightning and thunder. Then the rain started coming down hard, distorting the light from the orange streetlamp across the street. I sighed. I didn't like thunder, but I liked the sound of the rain. At least I had a roof over my head and a soft bed with very pink sheets.

Mom would be home in eighteen days and counting. At this point I had skipped two grades. I was confident I could figure out how to survive until Mom returned. I would make it work.

Then the streetlamp started flickering, and there was a glimmer of gold letters in the bookcase. It was a torn world atlas. I tried to ignore it, but I couldn't, and so I crept down from the top bunk to look something up, and I found it: Ascension Island was a volcanic island in the South

Atlantic Ocean, between Africa and Brazil. Somehow, knowing that made the nightmare hurt a little less.

We woke the next morning for school, and the house was full of breakfast smells. My stomach gurgled and grumbled as I dressed and hurried after the other kids to the kitchen.

They had bacon and eggs.

Dolly presented me the steak from last night. Still cold from the fridge. She said, "That's your breakfast," and I wanted to die. The fat was cold and hard, and the meat was stiff. I told Dolly I couldn't eat it.

"We'll see," she said, smirking. "That's fine. Get to school."

I rushed to school. As soon as the lunch bell rang, I realized she didn't pack me a lunch. I had no money. I was hungry. I felt like an orphan, watching everyone else feast. The rest of class was a blur.

After school, I opened the fridge, but Dolly slammed it closed. "Dinner is in a couple of hours. We'll eat then."

It was excruciating. It took me a long time to get through my homework.

At dinner, I got the same ice-cold steak and water. Everyone else had a cheesy casserole, bread with a tub of margarine they passed around, and apple pie for dessert. Dolly watched me, intently. No one else dared to look my way. I was only allowed to leave the table after they were done.

Her husband carried on like nothing was wrong.

After we shut the light and went to bed, Cindy whispered, "Just eat the steak and she'll stop."

"I can't," I whispered back.

"Just do it. Even if you have to throw up after."

"I just can't."

"You can't keep this up." It was the last thing Cindy ever said to me. The next night she got caught trying to sneak me food. Dolly's kids stopped talking to me. I was moved to a couch. They punished Cindy, and she never looked at me again.

Dolly set that steak out for three straight days. By then, it had maggots, and Dolly threw it away. I thought I had won a victory.

I was wrong. She still forced me to sit at the table for meals; everyone got food but me. Dolly excused me after everyone else finished, and I was furious, counting down the days until Mom came home. But I was starving, and I devised a plan.

After the second day, I started scavenging at school. Kids are always trading food and throwing out what they don't want. I was never tuned into it before. I never had to.

I'd quietly watch them eat. When they threw away their lunch bags, if no one was watching, I would get it. Kids throw a lot away.

My classmates weren't openly hostile, just cold and unfriendly. I didn't fit in with a lot of the other students. The coolness of skipping grades was lost on me. I was two years younger than my classmates. One morning, I was in second grade . . . by that afternoon, I was a fourth grader. They were bigger than me, but not more mature. To say it was awkward would be an understatement. On top of that was my racial complexity. Not being black or white was a hot button for adults, and we were at an age where kids mostly say and believe what their parents do, and much of it wasn't nice. Kids have no filter. My classmates couldn't figure me out, so they avoided me. The last of my friends had just Permanent Commission Stationed (a.k.a. PCS—a military term for when you relocate to a new military base) back to the states, and I came back from recess to find a diaper on my desk with the word "genius" written on it in marker.

I looked around, and the mean girls in the front row were snickering. When the teacher came in, she looked right at me and the diaper, ignored it, and started writing assignments on the board.

I sighed, sat down, and shoved that diaper in my desk, certain no one would help.

I ate out of the garbage for over two weeks while I continued without breakfast or dinner. At that point, it was survival, and I became good at it.

Weekends were awful; I could only scavenge on school days. In town, the Germans kept a wary eye on Americans from the base, and I learned the hard way that base-housing trash got picked up while I was at school. My first weekend with Dolly, I snuck to the kitchen late at night and there were locks on the fridge and pantry doors. After that, I scavenged as much as I could at school, hiding any unopened food I found to make a weekend stash.

I grew stealthy. Eating unobserved, removing all evidence of my food, wrappers, and crumbs like I was never there.

The day Mom came to get me, I was packed and happily waiting on the front porch ready to go. I had never looked so forward to something before. I was finally free. I latched onto her until she had to disengage from my hug.

"I'm happy to see you too," she said. "Let's go."

I just nodded. I didn't know what to say. I didn't know if I was going to have to stay with Dolly again. I was terrified to say anything, but it was over.

Mom was back, and we were going home. She couldn't drive away fast enough.

Mom was blah blah blahing about this and that as we pulled away. I didn't listen as I felt the warmth of her voice wash over me. It wasn't until she got to, "Oh, how was staying with Dolly?" that my stomach growled. Loud.

She laughed. "Do you want to pick up something—"

"McDonald's!" I yelled without letting her finish the statement.

She nodded and drove us thirty miles to get there. McDonald's was a big deal in Germany in the 1980s, and I ate like there was no tomorrow. I was twenty nuggets in and on my second hamburger when my mom went, rather flippantly, "God, I've never seen you eat like this. Must be a growth spurt."

"I haven't eaten in two weeks," came out, matter-of-factly, from my mouth full of food, like I had said water is wet, or the sky is blue. I remember feeling put out that I had to waste valuable eating time telling her that.

"Sweetie, seriously. Just because you don't like—"

"This isn't a joke!" Tears soaked my fries, and the entire story poured out. Raw meat. Then no food. Forced to watch everyone else eat. Scavenging for food out of the garbage.

"Wait. What did you just say?" It was her sternly worded tone. I rarely heard it. It meant that if this was a joke, it was over, and I was to come clean immediately.

"Really?" It might have sounded cold or mechanical, I don't know; in that moment, my mind was all about eating.

"I said I haven't eaten in weeks, and if I don't get the food in now, I'll have to—" I stopped when I finally met her eyes. I saw profound things on her face I had never seen before. She was stunned, for sure. Her face morphed through shock to disbelief to seething anger as she appraised me. It was the awful truth, her worst fears, and she knew it.

The look on her face was not the professional demeanor of an Air Force officer rooting out fact or managing a crisis. It was the face of a mother with a broken heart.

Everything she had fought to protect me from. Everything she feared. I had only seen my mother cry once before, and it broke me. I didn't mean to hurt her feelings. The impact of my words never dawned on me. I never forgot that she was a single parent who had to work and travel. She was military. Her job was to protect people who couldn't protect themselves. She did everything she could, but she couldn't protect me.

We cried together. My anger faded away, but the hurt stayed with me, exposed and raw. They were hard lessons for both of us. I discovered first-hand how it felt when adults betray a child's trust, when the security they inherently believe in is shattered, and how utterly powerless I felt to do anything about it.

I learned that even though I could still stand my ground and survive, not saying it happened when it happened hurt even more.

The look on my mom's face was etched into my mind forever. She's the strongest woman I have ever known, and I watched her cry at McDonald's in her perfectly pressed uniform, saying she was so sorry until it hurt to hear. People she had trusted and paid to take care of me, when she couldn't do it herself, had hurt and abused me. She cried. I cried. I don't think she ever got over that betrayal.

I will never forget the look in her eyes. This was a life lesson I didn't fully comprehend until maturity: that evil has no regulator; that there are people who will prey upon the innocent, the helpless, and those with no one to intercede on their behalf. It is the infinite fuel of my warrior spirit and is cemented into my foundations.

CHAPTER 2

DOGS WITHOUT WHISTLES

"Hold fast to dreams / For if dreams die /
Life is a broken-winged bird / That cannot fly."
—Langston Hughes[1]

Dolly's family got orders and left Germany shortly after Mom got back. I never heard what happened, but the moving truck came, they were gone, and that night a new family moved into their house. Mom seemed pleased, and I eventually learned to eat red meat again. The new family had an American dad, a German mother named Hilda, a daughter named Sarah. She was a few grades behind me, but we were the same age, walked to the same school, and grew to be friends.

I didn't speak German when we arrived in Germany. I learned a few words to get by and I learned a few more from what the locals muttered under their breath as we walked to and from school. The Germans off-base didn't like their American neighbors, but they loved the money the base brought into town. Still, they were openly hostile to us.

I learned that *Amerikanische schweine und scheisse* meant "American pigs and shits," and they divided us kids into dark, light, and other. I looked dark to them, so I quickly learned *negerin*, *schwarzer*, and *mohr* were variations of *neger*, which is exactly what it sounds like. I was called *mohrenkof*—a chocolate-covered marshmallow—by the adults I passed on the street who didn't like *neger*-kind in their town every morning and late afternoon when they were out shopping for dinner.

There was no distinction between innocent children and Americans who were naïve to the customs and cultures of others. When pointing and muttering wasn't enough, they did worse. Their hatred of Americans was deep-seated, and children often pay for adult choices and mistakes. My grandfather used to say, "Children's shoulders aren't broad enough to bear adult consequences," but that is exactly what I did.

One lady—a fast-aging, mid-thirties brunette in heels—always stood in her yard, cursing and spitting in disgust at us on our way back from school. She had a mean German Shepard that was always snarling and barking at us from behind her gate or pulling at its leash as it lunged at us. It was big, loud, and scary.

We lived on base but went to the American military school in the neighboring city of Kaiserslautern. School was a mile-and-a-half walk from the base through a dark, overgrown forest, then over a rickety, rusted, green bridge that spanned a busy freeway. We called the bridge the Green Monster. It swayed and creaked as you crossed it. I hated that bridge, and the older kids would make fun of me for always running across it as fast as I could. In my mind, it made sense. If I could just get three-quarters of the way across, if it collapsed into the street, my momentum would carry me the rest of the way over the bridge. On either side of the forest and bridge were villages with cobblestone roads and picture-book medieval houses full of Germans who hated Americans.

Because of the growing military tension, we weren't allowed to walk to school alone. It used to be just me and Sarah, but then a kid named Kelvin (whom I couldn't stand) joined us. I found out later that my mother arranged Kelvin to be an added safety-in-numbers protection.

Kelvin had a massive crush on me and even after telling him to go away, he wouldn't stop following me around. I didn't get it. I was a tomboy. He was the class clown. He wasn't good at school or sports, and he was annoying. I was as mean to him as I could be, but Kelvin latched onto us, saying he loved me, and Sarah thought it was hysterical. I didn't find it humorous at all, not one bit. It was killing me, but after my pleas to my mother to remove him were unsuccessful, I had to accept it. Thankfully, he mostly stopped with the kitten eyes. And ultimately, the three of us were stuck with each other.

One day as soon as we got off the Green Monster, we heard a dog barking. We had just entered into the forest and still had half a mile to get to the backside of base housing. It sounded different this time. "Guys," I said. "Is the barking getting closer?"

"No," they said together, which was annoying, but we were walking through a dark stretch of forest with a barking dog we couldn't see somewhere nearby, and that made us edgy. We picked up the pace, and the snarls got louder. We broke into a section of tall, thick pine trees like giant telephone poles. I looked back, and the big German Shepard that was always barking at us was charging us. Foaming at the mouth. Growling. Almost on us.

There was a tree with sharp, broken-off branches leaning a little over that we could climb, and I was an expert tree climber. "There," I shouted. I pushed Sarah onto the trunk. Pulled myself up behind her. Clawed at the branches. The dog snarled and snapped at us, so close I could smell its hot breath. I felt it on my legs and back. It was terrifying.

Kelvin was right behind me, but he wasn't a great tree climber.

Sarah started crying, "What do I do?" and froze.

The sharp branches cut my hands. I pushed at her to keep going, but she wouldn't budge. I tried to push her higher, but she had a death grip on the trunk, and I wasn't strong enough.

I left bloody palm marks on her back.

Kelvin was screaming, "Help! Help me!"

He was kicking at the dog and clinging to a low branch.

The dog was biting at his legs, trying to get a grip on him.

I got the best foothold I could. We grabbed each other's arm and pulled.

He made it to the next branch. Higher up the tree.

Kelvin was screaming. Sarah was crying. One last leg to get up.

One more pull and he'd be clear.

In the blink of an eye, the dog leaped. Its jaws latched on to Kelvin's right leg.

Kelvin screamed again. The snarling dog hung from him, shaking its whole body with all its weight. And Kelvin was gone. Pulled to the ground. The dog savaged him. Kelvin tried to crawl away. The snarling German Shepard was tearing chunks from his leg.

I shouted, "Help us!" Over and over. "Someone. Please. Help us!"

And someone came out of the dark woods into the pine grove where we were screaming, as the dog mauled Kelvin on the ground.

A silhouette became the woman who owned the dog. She looked like she was going to the spa. Leisurely walking toward us. Nice and relaxed, seemingly unphased by the brutality of her dog viciously attacking a grade-school boy.

She didn't even pretend to call the dog off. She just grabbed its collar and growled at it in German.

The dog released Kelvin and sat. The woman looked at the crying children with disgust. She examined the dog to make sure it was alright, glared at Kelvin, and, as though nothing had happened, she strolled away with her dog.

Kelvin was curled up, crying, and moaning. Sarah was still scared and frozen a quarter-way up the tree. We were all crying. Coaxing Sarah down and getting Kelvin up was hard.

Sarah and I were still sniffling when we got his arms around our shoulders to help Kelvin hop to base. It was a half mile away. It took forever. The sun was setting, and it was getting cold when we reached the back gate. We were exhausted, bleeding, and shaking. I called out, "Help us! This lady let her dog attack us. Kelvin's hurt." I could barely hear my voice.

But the military police heard my cries. Two of them raced us to the base hospital and called our parents.

Kelvin had bites everywhere, and when they cut away his pant legs, chunks were missing from his calf. I could see his bone. A nurse took Sarah and me to another room to have our scrapes and cuts cleaned and bandaged. We all got shots; Kelvin got a sedative and a lot of stitches and was snoring in a hospital bed when our parents arrived.

Sarah's mom and Kelvin's mom were crying. Kelvin's dad and my mom were furious. Mom was a major in the Air Force at the time, and Kelvin's father was a captain; that was a really big deal at the military base. They went to an office past the nurse's station with a doctor and people from security forces. There was a loud discussion between our parents, the base commander, and the military police commander.

I said goodbye to Sarah and her mom when they left.

Kelvin's dad said, "Raven, honey. I need you to show me the house where this dog came from." I was tired and nervous, but he said, "I'll make sure you get home safely."

"We're coming too," my mom said. She brought a security detail. I recognized some of them as the dads of kids at my school.

My mother handled it. She didn't scream or yell, but when she was angry, it was brutal. She definitely had a reputation of being someone you didn't mess with. I never saw or heard that dog or the lady who owned it again.

We visited Kelvin at the hospital the next day. He joked around, but they couldn't discern if the dog had rabies. He had a painful recovery and was out of school for a week. I literally ran through the forest after that. It was a terrifying thing, and I had nightmares of big, howling, snapping dogs chasing me for a long time after.

The path through the woods was never an uneventful walk. Someone came through once a year and cleared the way, but by winter, the forest had reclaimed most of the path. Hidden branches and undergrowth grabbed your clothes, and slippery moss grew. When the sun went down early, it was dreadful coming home from school. It was like a hike in a haunted forest.

Everything seemed to get darker and grayer. Kelvin's family got orders and moved away, and I relived being chased by that dog and the blood and our screams every time I walked that path to school. It was traumatic. I felt like a lightning rod for everybody's hate walking through those villages. I could feel it. Even on base, I could feel it. It was subtle. It wasn't always there, but when it was, it came out in the tone of their voices, and I could see it in their eyes.

People refused to salute my mom because they resented an officer who was a person of color. Sometimes I said, "Mommy, he's supposed to salute." And she would say, "His issues are bigger than his honor." She had to be more because she was treated like less.

We've come a long way. Of course, racism still exists, but I'm not hypersensitive to it or looking for it so I can instantly go, "Oh . . . racism. This is racist, that is racist." I don't live behind it, but I know what racism looks like. The difference is that military warriors raised me. I wasn't given a pass for victimhood, which is what I feel it's morphed into.

There's good and bad in everything, and I'm not a victim. I'm a survivor. There's a big difference. Racism is a layer of life I have to deal with. My mom used to always say everybody has something to deal with. Some people have speech impediments. Some have disabilities or are missing limbs. Some folks don't have parents or people they can look to who want the best for them. For some people, it's the color of their skin.

Everyone has something to overcome and deal with. The color of my skin happens to be one of mine. There are many days I have to deal with racism. The part I'd like for people to understand is that I don't get to decide which days those are.

Left-leaning extremists, safe in their ivory towers and gated communities, like to talk about dog whistles. They seem to hear them everywhere. It's the metaphor they use to describe the slightest hint of possible racism, exaggerating disagreements or stupidity as acts of violence. Dog whistles. They have no idea what it feels like to have a dog sicced on them because they're different and someone hates you for it. A dog whistle turns people into prey.

I'll never forget what it was like. Being hunted. The terror. No quarter. No surrender. The "failure is not an option" doctrine I was raised on was cemented then.

━━━━━

The Red Brigade was active across Europe, and after a series of train station and car bombings, Germans were feeling less safe and wanted more protection. As the Americans began capturing terrorists and sharing intelligence that reduced the risk of more attacks across Europe, the animus toward Americans lessened. One day, Americans are greedy, entitled elitists in their eyes; the next day, there's another bombing, and they ask, "Where are the Americans? Why aren't they helping more?"

After the 1981 Red Army Faction parking-lot bombing at Ramstein Air Base that wounded twenty-two airmen, there was a concerted effort between NATO, the US Air Force, and German authorities. Many security improvements were made in and around the base, and many of the subsequent assassination attempts and car bombings were unsuccessful. Their hostility toward us didn't end overnight, but we went from being cursed at and spit on to just being ignored as we walked to school.

By this time, I had a father. He is in my earliest memories and there were some eerie physical and behavioral similarities with us. He was my mother's boss, but they were the same rank and equals. Just as things were improving, we got orders to Berlin, and the moving truck came for us.

I was too young to understand what the Cold War was about, but in Germany, there were times I could feel the tension. My earliest memories are of hearing the word "communism." It was a big word and, like most military kids, I heard it daily. We were fighting communism. We were told our parents were fighting communism, and they were patriots. As a child, I understood communism was "over there," and my parents' job was to keep it from coming "over here."

Living in Berlin was different. After Nazi Germany was defeated in World War II, their capitol, Berlin, was divided and administered by the Allied Powers. Over time, all the Allies—except the Soviet Union—transferred control of Berlin back to Germany. They built a wall around their section, and that wall, known as the Berlin Wall, became the demarcation line between oppression and freedom.

The wall cut through neighborhoods and buildings. It divided Berlin and families into West and East, free and not. The air force stationed us in Berlin, and we lived on the free side in West Berlin. Vivid graffiti covered our side of the Wall, and West Berliners seemed to live for every moment.

My parents worked across the wall in communist East Berlin, and sitters were hard to find. I often accompanied them, and that was a big deal. We needed special papers, our passports were triple checked, and I had to be on access lists on both the US Army and East German sides of Checkpoint Charlie. I never got to do anything exciting or tour the city, only walk from the checkpoint to Mom's work. They watched us, and we had to follow a specific route without deviations. Parts of the Berlin Wall weren't very tall at all. Actually, there were two walls—an inner wall and an outer wall—with a kill zone of landmines, floodlights, snipers, and guard towers between them. Parts of the free West and communist East Berlin were closer together, others widely separated, but each side was a different world.

They strung barbwire in layers near and above the Wall. Guards patrolled. In East Berlin, no kids played in the street. Except for the soldiers, people rarely walked together and when they did, they didn't talk. No one held hands. No one smiled. Ever. The communist East Berlin was a prison within a prison: a robotic existence carried out under the unrelenting watch of heavily armed soldiers.

I could see buildings in East Berlin from the freedom of the West side built to make bold statements to the world. Even through the damage, neglect, and grime, you could still see their grandeur. They were the exceptions. Most of the buildings were a dull gray or buff blur of anonymous old stone and concrete buildings, with no graffiti brightening the East side of the wall.

There were two US Embassies in Germany: one in Bonn, a city in the West; the other in East Berlin. Usually there was a car waiting for us a few streets past the checkpoint. Sometimes it was a thirty-minute walk. After more checkpoints, crossing through restricted access areas with card readers, my mother would settle me in a room where I could do homework, read, or sleep until she returned.

Sometimes she'd come back and take me out to lunch. We'd walk by Soviet-era buildings, passing dreary, cookie-cutter people wearing the same trench coat and trousers before going into nearly empty restaurants where conversations stopped when we entered, replaced by furtive glances, then whispers.

Everything was old. From the few cars on the street to the patched shoes people wore. Mom paid for lunch in deutsche marks. Two sandwiches with potato salad and drinks cost less than I paid for candy on the free side. I didn't understand. I asked my mom how it could be so cheap. She said, "This is what communism is. Control and suffering for power."

Everyone there was poor. Everything we saw was poor. Those people had nothing, not even a voice. They were controlled at gunpoint. They were dehumanized and empty.

That was my experience with communism until a few months before we were to PCS from Germany back to the states.

As we got new duty orders and prepared to return to America, my mother decided to purchase a nice German sports car. Perhaps she had gotten a little too spoiled driving on the autobahn with no speed limit because, on the free side, she commissioned the first-ever black Porsche 944 with a burgundy interior, since it was cheaper to buy in Germany and ship home. Only red Porsches were made, never black; no one had ever asked for a black one before. She paid $19,000 for a car that would have cost $26,500 to buy in the states.

My mother driving an expensive sports car around prompted inquiries into her finances and investments, but until the internal investigation was done, she was constantly interrogated about her ability to afford such a luxury. For her, it was a status symbol that represented everything she didn't have growing up. She was proud of the deal she got on it, and she loved that car more than anything else. Until the investigation was over and she was cleared of wrongdoing, she worked in one of the taller buildings in free Berlin. It had a rickety, elevated parking garage that made groaning noises I didn't like when we drove through it. I'd walk there after school, finish my schoolwork before she got out of work, and then we'd go home together. We were talking more, and it was nice.

The view from the breakroom and parking garage allowed me to see inside the Wall—over the barbwire, between the machine gun towers— into what looked like a prison yard. It was rare to see people there who weren't soldiers with guns on patrol or marching troops doing drills.

Even though I was safe in a military building on the free side of Berlin, it was scary to see. It was cold enough to see your breath, but the room I was in had a portable electric heater that made the small room warm and me sleepy.

My homework was done, and I was nodding off, so I got up to stretch when my mom came in to take us home. She had just started the car when I heard, "Damn."

"Mom. What's the matter?"

"Forgot something. Be right back."

The sun was setting, and the yellow floodlights around East Berlin were turning on.

From my vantage point in the car, I could see over the barbwire into the prison yard. When the lights came on, a guy was standing there. He had a hat and something covering his ears. I remember he was wearing purple, fingerless gloves that seemed to glow in the yellow light.

He was alone. Intently staring at the Wall across from him. Seemingly oblivious to the situation escalating around him.

Soldiers were converging on him, weapons drawn.

But he stood there motionless. Not a smidgen of emotion on his face.

I don't know what he was thinking or doing there, but he was calm as the troops closed in on him, and it captivated me.

Suddenly, he took off, sprinting for the Wall.

I could hear the faraway warble of an alarm. A megaphone, in German, barked orders.

The only word I could make out was *halt*.

I watched until the guy got too close to the Wall, and I couldn't see him anymore.

The soldiers followed him past my view.

The megaphoned-German shouting got louder, and his purple gloves erupted through the barbwire at the top of the Wall. He was pulling himself up. Scaling the Wall.

He was almost over.

He was smiling.

Then, the guard towers lit up, there were *pops*, and he was gone.

I looked closer. His purple gloved arm still showed through the wire. *Pop. Pop. Pop. Pop. Pop.*

His arm gestured like he was waving.

There was blood in the yellow light.

His arm slid back behind the Wall.

His shredded, gloved hand hung there, caught in the wire above East Berlin. Not moving. Even the purple color was gone.

I couldn't process what happened.

Mom threw open the car door. "Oh, my God."

I couldn't look away.

She pulled my head to her chest. When I couldn't see him anymore, it hit me. I felt sick. "They killed him."

We slowly descended the steep parking lot ramps, and when Mom turned onto the street, she wrung every bit of performance out of that sports car and drove like a maniac all the way home.

The flat was cold. She closed the door and turned up the heat. "You okay?"

"Not really."

"You want to talk about it?"

"Not really."

"Okay. When you're ready."

We went to our rooms. She closed the door. I sat in the corner by the ticking radiator, my arms wrapped around my legs, squeezing them to my chest. Shaking despite the heat embracing me.

A few hours later, she came into my room. "I'm sorry you had to see that."

"Why did they kill him?"

She sat at the end of the bed across from me. "Because communists control their people with guns."

"Why didn't he just leave through the gate we used to go through?"

She sighed. "Because they wouldn't let him. I know it's hard to understand, but they couldn't control him if he had the freedom to leave."

"I don't understand."

"I know. But this is why freedom is so important. It's your most valuable thing."

"So I can come and go where I want?"

"That. And so you're free to be who you want to be, and who you are. We have that, they don't. And it's one reason I wear a uniform. I fight to make sure no one will take our freedom away from us."

A few weeks later, Germany was behind us, and we were flying to Wright-Patterson AFB in Ohio, but I never forgot Berlin. I never forgot that man trying to make it over the Wall. I never forgot his face when he made it to the top, and I'll never forget what his country did to him. His government decided they knew better than their people, and they killed him.

A glimmer of freedom cost him his life.

I saw that man die because he'd had enough. Death was a better option.

That was communism.

People want freedom. Some will sacrifice anything and everything to get it. No one escapes persecution by fleeing to communist or socialist countries to live under the tyranny of control, abdicating your inalienable rights to the government; being told where to go, what to eat, how to live. No one illegally enters Russia, China, or Argentina to secure a better life for their family.

What happens when we discover tyranny here? What do we do?

Who will fight against it?

The answer is: I will. I will do what I was raised to do. I will fight to preserve the freedom that so many gave their fortunes—and, in some cases, their lives—to protect. When God calls, I will answer.

CHAPTER 3

WAKE-UP CALL

"Darkness cannot drive out darkness; only light can do that.
Hate cannot drive out hate; only love can do that."
—Martin Luther King, Jr.[1]

A few years later, the Wall came down. East Germans were free. Families torn apart by communism reunited.

I still think about that man. Did he have a family? He faced death to be free. I wonder what he left behind. I think about the freedoms we take for granted, especially when I'm campaigning on the road. I'm overwhelmingly grateful that I grew up in America.

A few years ago, I was on the cusp of the biggest corporate sponsorship with my business, Race2theRaven, and we were in negotiations to turn one of our projects into a reality TV show. Paul had retired from the Air Force and was flying for the airlines, and we had two beautiful children in school.

We worked hard and moved into a house I hated so our kids could go to the best school in Huntington Beach, California. Most of my childhood was just me and my mom bouncing from base to base until she connected with my dad, the coolest dad in the world, before we left Germany. Even after they were together, I was skipping grades and transferring schools, and I never got to graduate with a class I started with. When Paul and I had Patience and Major, we wanted them to have the stability I didn't have growing up. We did everything you're supposed to do and more. I ticked every box, and even some extra, to win Mother of the Year. You know. Hate the house, check. Husband gone all the time, check. The noise of the nearby elementary school, check. Big black widow spider as a bad omen on the fence, check.

It was an exciting time in our lives and the first time we'd house hunted so our kids could attend a particular school. There was an extremely long waitlist for those not zoned for that school, and we couldn't risk them not getting in.

To cement our kids' places in the most desired school in the district, we let go of the beautiful home we wanted and instead bought an over-priced house I was highly unimpressed with.

Our oldest, Patience, is an energetic, athletic, and stunningly beautiful Caucasian and Native American girl with a heart as big as the state. When we bought the house, she was eight years old, in the third grade, and loved school, her friends, and stuffed animals. Now, she's a TV starlet with three representing agencies and a portfolio of high-profile work that includes commercials for Disney and Ugg. She is popular, but best of all, she is kind.

Major is smart and gentle, but even in first grade he was easily a foot taller than his peers. Adults and kids treated him like he was older than he was, and that made him shy and withdrawn.

Our unimpressive house had a backyard that faced the school, and we could see their lunch area from our kitchen. Occasionally, we'd glimpse our kids ducking under flying food or negotiating trades for the contents of their lunches. My stomach knotted the first time I saw it. Then I let it go and smiled as I watched their lunches trade hands. I'd come a long way.

━━━━━

The call came late afternoon. Paul had just gotten home. I looked up from my work. It was the school.

"May I speak to Mr. or Mrs. Harrison?"

"Yes. Speaking."

"This is Ms. Alcott from Franklin Elementary. Patience is fine, but we need you to come to the school immediately. There was an incident."

"An incident? Where is my daughter?" I said, violently motioning to Paul as I slid on my shoes. "Is she hurt? What's wrong?"

There was a pause. "Patience isn't hurt, but we need you to come right away."

"School's out in ten minutes! What happened?"

"It would be best if you picked her up now."

"We're on our way."

Click.

The call set off my alert sirens. My head was full of terrible potential scenarios.

When we got to the school, Major saw us before we saw him. He bopped over, appearing with an excited, "Tada! Hi, Mommy. Hi, Daddy. Did you miss me? We should get snickerdoodles ."

"I always miss you. But we have a meeting with Patience's teacher."

"Ohhh. Is she in trouble?"

"Why would you ask that?"

"'Cause she never has to stay after school."

Just then, our friend Jenn was coming to get her kids, and she agreed to take him. "Go home with Jenn, baby. We can get snickerdoodles later."

"'Kay."

We watched Major trot away and walked up to her teacher, unsure of what to expect. Patience had never been in trouble before. The rational part of me kept saying it could be anything and to wait for the facts. You're not heading to the hospital. You got this.

But the mom part of me needed to see that she wasn't laid out somewhere, bleeding.

All the kids were departing, and Patience was nowhere to be found. It was the usual after-school chaos, and we were in the middle of it, looking for the principal, her teacher, or our daughter—or anyone who could tell us what happened. Our concern and anger were ratcheting up as we searched the thinning crowd.

We found Patience's teacher, Ms. Cantor, laughing and talking with someone I didn't recognize. I made a beeline for her.

When our eyes locked, she wrinkled her nose.

"Where's my daughter?"

She didn't answer. She turned away and said goodbye to her friend, grinned, and left.

After being called in and ignored by Patience's teacher, I skipped the pleasantries and demanded again, "Where is my daughter?"

"She's in detention."

"For what? What did she do?"

"She needs to rethink her choices," Ms. Cantor said, dismissively.

"What does that mean?"

I waited. She didn't answer, and I was done playing Twenty Questions. My fuse was short and lit. I had waited long enough. When she still didn't answer, I pushed past her. "I don't have time for this. I'm going to get my daughter now."

"Oh no. You can't go back there. You have to wait here."

That was highly suspicious and made no sense to us. "I'm her mother. Why don't you want us back there?"

She stomped her sparkly rainbow clogs. "You're not supposed to go back there unescorted." Her voice shrill. "Wait!"

I kept walking. I figured she'd follow. Instead, she rushed to the office, like she was calling for backup. Which was weird. It wasn't like I was storming Normandy. School was over. I was getting my daughter.

Paul was my wingman with a stoic look on his face, scanning the hall. Both of us tried to process what happened. Recently I had told him something felt off at the school, but I couldn't put my finger on what. Paul's a pilot. He's calm and logical. Strategic. A planner. He'd listen then say, "But what exactly is wrong?" I didn't have an answer. Only a sense that something wasn't right, and we dismissed it. New house. New school. New people and places. We just weren't used to our new life yet. Nothing is perfect. There were red flags, but we believed the dream and wanted it to be real.

Patience's friend Sophie was there, nervously guarding the classroom door. She ran up to me and hugged me tighter than usual. She was shaking. When she looked up, she was crying.

"Baby, what happened?"

"Miss Raven, they grabbed her by the collar when she tried to go out for last recess," Sophie's voice cracked, "and I wasn't allowed to stay in class with her and—"

Rage washed over me. *They did what?* She looked so small and scared. I kneeled. "You did good, Sophie. I'm so glad Patience has a friend like you. I'll take it from here. Go ahead home, baby."

Sophie sniffled, rubbed her eyes, and nodded.

"You are so very brave. Tell your mom I'll call her later."

I walked in with Paul. Patience was sitting at her desk, clutching a piece of paper, alone in the classroom, crying hysterically. Her eyes red and swollen. She was hyperventilating.

"Baby, what's wrong?" We raced to her. She met us halfway.

She couldn't answer. Patience held onto me, trying to catch her breath.

She was terrified. I checked for marks on her neck. There were red splotches on her neck, but I couldn't tell if they were hives or something else. There was no faculty in sight to explain, and all I could do was hold her. "Mommy and Daddy are here. You're okay. We're here now. We got you."

That's what I said, but my heart was pounding. *My God, my baby. What happened?*

I was livid. We still didn't know why.

When her breathing finally deepened and slowed, she deflated in my arms. She didn't look up until I peeled her teeny fingers from my arm. When she did, I could see it in her eyes.

The panic was gone. She looked from Paul to me. She could see she was safe again, but her gaze broke my heart.

What remained in her glossy, wide, beautiful eyes was betrayal.

I could feel her hurt.

Whatever had happened had shaken her to her core.

What Patience said next cut me deep. "I'm so sorry Mommy, I—" she started sobbing again and wiping away tears with her little hands.

I knew that look on her face. I said the same thing when I was small.

I didn't protect her. I failed her. It was visceral. It tasted like rotten meat in my mouth, and I wanted to throw up. I was back to Dolly, to that place where my mother sat when I told her, looking into her eyes, her *anguish* that she failed me.

It was an overwhelming moment for me because Patience was hurting, and you never know what will come back for you from your childhood. It was like I was that eight-year-old girl looking in her eyes again. My mother knowing she didn't protect me on her watch.

Me knowing that whatever had happened to Patience happened on my watch.

She asked me, "Are you mad?"

"At you? No, baby. Not even a little."

She was a sensitive child. Her chin quivered. Patience was trying to tell me why she was crying alone in a classroom. Why she wasn't allowed to leave. While her teacher laughed and carried on until we asked her what happened with our daughter and then she ran away.

That's when the door swung open. Three of them: the principal, her teacher, and the office administrator who called us. The "responsible" adults who called us to get our daughter immediately had finally arrived. I expected them to try to justify the mess they had clearly created, but they didn't even do that, or explain why they left Patience alone. They just stood there, looking arrogantly perplexed, like the Three Stooges.

My mom was the nicest, most caring person, until someone crossed her—then she was ferocious. It's a trait I definitely inherited from her, likely from the long line of Native American warriors in my family. I am very mindful of my temper and my responses, largely from being taught to expect the consequences of my actions.

This was the first time in my life I chose to obliterate my filters. I was done waiting, and I exploded. "What happened?"

At five-foot-ten, Patience's teacher, Ms. Cantor, was used to towering over the kids in her class, and when Paul stepped up to meet them, she clearly didn't enjoy looking up at him.

Mr. Deveraux, the school's flamboyant principal who, until that day, always held my husband's hand overlong after every shake.

And his secretary, Ms. Alcott, whose phone voice I won't forget.

Seeing the optics of a now hysterical nine-year-old girl crying in the room and confronting angry parents, they did what bureaucrats do: tried to ignore my question, regain control, and act like nothing happened.

I had always moderated myself and given them the benefit of the doubt, but they had clearly mistaken my kindness and respect for them as weakness.

They crossed a line. They harmed my baby. It was war.

"You have fifteen seconds to tell me what you did to my daughter before I level this place." I wanted to hold her, but Mama was erupting. I crouched and gave her a kiss. "Go to Daddy now."

With a nod, Patience was in Paul's arms. She wrapped herself around him so tight it left marks. Safe in his arms, her quiet sobs turned into wailing tears. We'd never seen Patience like that. Paul hovered between wary and furious, and I glared. "I'm tiring of repeating myself. What did you do?"

Principal Deveraux said, "I'm sorry she's so upset."

"You still haven't told us why, and our daughter is hysterical. Be very careful with what you say next."

"We should go to my office and discuss matters there."

"You have ten seconds left. Talk."

Principal Deveraux cleared his throat. "Ms. Cantor will explain," and Ms. Cantor looked like she'd been thrown under the bus.

"Well, we were . . . we had a mock election today."

I'm looking at her like *you better make this good.*

"Get to the damn point. And get there fast," Paul said to the shock of everyone. He was the cool, collected one. He was rocking Patience, and she was settling down, but his eyes were laser locked with the principal, until Principal Deveraux looked away.

I realized I had put myself between them and my daughter. "You're studying civics? Because I don't remember hearing anything about you teaching civics in the third grade."

Confusion spread across her face like she wasn't expecting that question.

"Okay, so you were studying civics. Again, what happened?"

"Well, we voted today. The kids all voted, and Patience voted for Trump."

I'm not kidding. Paul and I leaned in and waited for the rest of it. But that was it, and Ms. Cantor looked like she'd just told a joke, and when it bombed, she didn't know what to do.

"So let me get this straight: you had a mock election. Different kids voted for different candidates, and that's it? You gave my daughter detention and called us to get her ASAP because you didn't like the way a third grader voted?"

Match meet fuse.

The teacher continued, "She is the only one in the class—no, the school—who voted for Trump. You must understand, if she's making these kinds of choices, what will she do in a few years? She must learn social responsibility now."

"She's eight, she can't vote for anyone! That was it? You do realize Trump really is the president," I said. "You understand that, don't you? That's kind of how it works."

Ms. Cantor actually snarled. "Well, what do you tell your daughter then about *that* man?"

"I told my daughter the truth. That, in an election, sometimes you get what you want, and sometimes you don't. Sometimes you get the person you want, sometimes you don't. This time I did. Then I tell her we're lucky to live in America, where despite our differences, after four or eight years there's a peaceful transfer of power when the people decide who they want next as president. That's how our republic works. You don't get to just make shit up and force kids to go along with it. Which is apparently what you've been doing."

"It's a travesty."

Fuse meet dynamite. "What? Freedom? Are you fucking crazy?" I lost it. I have never dropped an f-bomb so loud in my entire life. "I was in Berlin before the Wall came down. I've seen what happens to people when you take away their rights, their choice. What the hell is wrong with you? You have no idea how good you've got it. And largely thanks to my husband and parents putting themselves in harm's way for your right to be idiots."

"Mrs. Harrison, language," said Principal Deveraux.

I closed the distance between me and him, and he recoiled. "And you allowed this? Punishing a little girl for voting, in America? You didn't like the way Patience voted, so you destroy her faith in teachers. And you're okay with that? This is a school, not some twisted social experiment."

"Mrs. Harrison, you need to calm down."

"I am not one of your students, thank God. Don't tell me what I need to do! I need to calm down?" Has telling someone that ever worked in the history of ever? "You know what? Let me tell you what I need. I need you and your ilk to never be around children again. None of you. Ever. I need to know when I entrust my kids in your care that they are safe and learning how to read, write, and problem solve. You know, things that actually prepare them for their future. And I need you to understand that you are failing as educators. You aren't teaching them how to think, you're trying to control what they think. It's disgusting."

"This school will not encourage racism and—" I cut him off.

"Are you really going to play the race card with me to defend this? You're going to lecture a minority woman on racism? Let's think about what your job is. Is it the three R's, or is it mass indoctrination and creation of sheep?"

Mount Raven erupting was causing a stir, and the remaining people in the building were gathering at the classroom door. "Your job is to teach reading, writing, arithmetic, history, problem solving . . ."

At first, the audience emboldened Principal Deveraux and Ms. Cantor. They played to them, smugly wrapping themselves in an air of responsible authority. "We are simply protecting our students." He was purposefully vague about what happened, making it seem like the entire issue was my fault because I was out of line, and I wasn't having it.

"Don't even try to play the responsible educator. Patience didn't break a rule, or not do her work, or get into a fight, and she wasn't rude or disrespectful to anyone. You grabbed my daughter by the collar, took away her recess, isolated her in an empty classroom, and punished her because, in a mock election, she voted for President Trump," I continued, and the crowd's mood changed. They weren't on the sidelines anymore, and started muttering questions the principal didn't like:

"They really did that to Patience?"

"Detention because of how she voted? That's not right."

"Your job is to educate our children," I said. "You do that by teaching what you told us you were teaching, not by bullying kids who don't believe what you want. A nine-year-old girl made up her own mind in the social experiment on government that you sanctioned, and you hurt her for it. That's not education. That's how the Taliban treats kids."

Principal Deveraux put on a smile and told the other parents, "We're done here. The school is locking up. Ms. Alcott will walk you out." When they were gone, he shut the door.

While he was disentangling himself from the parents, Patience came over, looking nervously at the principal and her teacher, and tapped my arm.

Patience put a wet, crumpled piece of paper in my hand. Then ran back into her father's arms. It was still warm from her tears.

Her teacher had the audacity to try to snatch the paper from me.

I swatted her hand away. She glared.

"Lay another hand on me and you'll *lose* it!"

"Mrs. Harrison!"

"You seem pretty worked up," I said, gently peeling open the wad of paper that looked like crushed, wet origami. "What is this?"

They didn't answer.

I read the creased worksheet.

Their frowns deepened, and I backed up to Paul.

"You gave my daughter this for detention? You actually did this?"

"Raven, what is it?" Paul asked, tensing up against me. There was a growl in his voice.

I held the paper up to him, and he took it in his Patience-free hand.

I didn't want him to think I was exaggerating.

Paul's the pilot. He's the analytical one. There's always a rational explanation for everything. I could hear his teeth grind. I think he was trying to make sure it wasn't her handwriting or trying to validate that it wasn't as horrible as it seemed, but it was what it was.

Paul read the detention assignment aloud.

"Please write a hundred times neatly in cursive, 'Hillary is the real president and Trump is an ass.'"

"Wow," I said, stunned they had the arrogance to take it so far in school. "So this is what you call teaching civics?"

Paul was shaking his head in disbelief. As a pilot, you always prepare for the worst-case scenario. This was it. It wasn't as bad as we feared; it was worse. Way worse. It was broken trust. In Paul's mind, people just went to school to learn. Then he looked at me, and he said, "Raven, get her stuff. Get all her things. Let's get out of here."

I couldn't agree more.

I started emptying Patience's desk, and her teacher grabbed a book I pulled out of my hand and said, "That belongs to the school. You can't have it."

I immediately pulled it back from her hand. "You obviously aren't using it, and you can't teach. Or stop me from taking home things I paid for. Stay away from me. Stay away from my kids. I'll make this easy for you," I said, turning to Principal Deveraux. "We're withdrawing our kids from this school now. And we'll need their records and any evidence they ever set foot in this indoctrination camp you're calling a school."

The principal said, "That is unfortunate," without sounding like he meant it. "Perhaps this is for the best. You can pick up their records from the office on Monday. I can have everything ready for you then."

He smiled.

I smiled. "You'll have them for me now."

"Mrs. Harrison," he said, overdramatically emphasizing every syllable. "I regret that Patience had a bad day and that you are upset. Truly, I do. But there are procedures to withdraw your child from school that we simply must follow."

"Like the procedures that require you to grab a minor child by the neck, or the procedures to never leave a distraught child unattended, Mr. Deveraux? Or teaching a curriculum you never notified parents about? But you clearly had no problem doing that," I said, frowning at Patience's tear-streaked face.

"Everything will be ready Monday."

"I'll keep this simple for you because it's obvious you still don't get what you've done: either bring me her transcripts and withdrawal papers now, or I call the police."

"And you would do that, for what?"

"Child abuse, obviously. Followed by a call to our lawyer and the news. Patience is a popular child model and actress. Her agencies will no doubt share what happened at your school with their affiliate media companies, and this will spread like wildfire.

"So what'll it be? We can leave with everything we need, and never see you again, or they'll have reporters queued up in front of the school when the police arrive. You decide."

I smiled.

He didn't. "Fine." His cordial, condescending veneer shattered with a sneer. Principal Deveraux growled and left for his office, with Ms. Cantor clogging after him.

I was shaking with rage. "Paul, would you help Patience with her backpack and the stuff in her cubby?" I said, emptying her desk.

We signed the forms to take Patience and Major out of that school and left with an envelope of records, an overflowing backpack, and Patience in between us, holding our hands.

When we got home, Patience asked, "Mommy? Do I have to go back there?"

"No, baby. You never have to go back there again."

———

Kids are resilient, especially when they shouldn't have to be. Patience eventually calmed down, but there was a sad emptiness in her swollen red eyes as she sat there, arms crossed and rocking, staring at nothing. Paul looked at me. "What do I do?"

"Play with her. If she doesn't want to play, just sit with her, and keep her company. Even if you don't say a word, she'll know she's safe."

That's what helped when I felt that way, and it killed me watching my daughter go through it now.

Patience melted into Paul until she was asleep, and he carried her to her room. Betrayal is having your world pulled out from under you by the people you trust.

It's trauma. It's a violation. Patience was innocent, and her school tried to strip that away because, in their eyes, she needed reeducation. They told her to choose, and when her choice didn't reflect what they wanted, they punished her; but she didn't fold, and she didn't give in to peer pressure. She cried because she didn't understand why there could only be one right answer in a vote, and she cried because her assignment included curse words she knew she wasn't allowed to use. She could have just changed her vote, but she didn't. Patience stood firm.

My mind replayed my trauma. Dolly's neglect, the humiliation of eating out of the trash to survive, being hunted by a dog who tore chunks from my friend. It replayed, and in each time, a part of me was taken away. In that moment, I was my daughter and my mother and me, hurt and betrayed and trying to figure out how I could make this right for Patience. To give her back the piece of her childhood she had lost that day.

I knew the loss I saw in my daughter's eyes, just as I knew what I would see in my eyes, looking back at me in a mirror. Betrayal always starts somewhere, and it always leaves its mark.

What did I miss?

Her backpack was overflowing, so I started there and dumped it out.

It was like the world's worst garage sale as I made piles of trash: abandoned things, ridiculously priced books, pencil stubs, and the remains of school supplies I'd just restocked.

I had meticulously organized their assignments and homework to keep on top of it. I went through Patience's third-grade curriculum and homework assignments, and there was nothing on civics or government. Then I compared it to the things I took from her desk.

I went through everything and every assignment. I was at it for hours.

It was like a punch in the gut.

They ran the school like a dirty business, with two sets of books for nearly every subject. Except for common core math, there were the books the kids could bring home with assignments that matched the syllabus Ms. Cantor had sent home for parents, and then there were books the students weren't allowed to bring home, filled with assignments quite different from those listed in the curriculum.

Until that point, I'd never heard of critical race theory (CRT) or social-emotional learning (SEL), but the assignments spelled out that black kids were victims and the children of victims, and white kids were oppressors and the children of oppressors. Assignments read like, "How do we address that violence? How do we make it right?"

I found a worksheet stating, "Native Americans were happy to build missions for early settlers. It taught them to reject their pagan ways and learn new skills," and I almost threw up. I also found LGBTQ+ books with graphic pictures and reading assignments that weren't on the class reading list. These are just a few examples of the differences I found.

It was 8:00 p.m., and my head hurt. I'd just finished stunning Paul with what our kids were learning about in school. It would have been unbelievable if it wasn't all laid out in front of us, and the effort the school had made to hide it from parents.

It was a shadow curriculum.

I was exhausted, but Patience came in, and when Paul told her there was pie . . . well, it was nice to see her smile again.

She and Paul returned with pie that looked more like mountains of whipped cream. While she excavated pie from the mountain, I held up the books we'd brought home.

Three of them were, "Oh, that's a school-only book. We're not allowed to bring those home."

When she looked like her old self again, I asked, "How you feeling?"

"I'm okay, Mommy. Ms. Cantor wanted me to write a lie, and the A-word, and those are things I'm not supposed to do. I voted for Trump, and when I wouldn't change it, she told me to stay at my desk and left mad. I'm sorry I got in trouble."

"You've got nothing to be sorry for, Punkin," Paul said, mussing her hair.

Patience gave me a big hug, and she goes, "You okay, Mommy?"

Kids are perceptive. "Yeah, baby." I didn't realize it was so late. I hugged her back, epically. "Now get some sleep. Tomorrow we have to find a new school."

"Good," Patience said, stopping at the door, "because I would vote for him again."

I had a new sense of vigilance and disgust for "educators" who lied about what they were teaching. Who turns kids against each other and against their parents with hidden agendas? Who smiles as they cast children in hateful roles of victim and oppressed that weren't true? That made kids feel bad about who they are? Who punishes children who disagree with their distorted views of how we've overcome our past and creates a world where systematic racism is still keeping people of color down because, poor us, we aren't capable of getting an ID or standing up for ourselves? Yet, somehow, the people also elected a black president for two terms without riots or rebellion. What they were teaching wasn't real.

They were teaching elementary school students that male and female were opinions, that sex didn't exist but was something fluid (despite biology and empirical, hard-science evidence saying that men and women *are* men and women, and the basis of humanity).

When I was researching Patience's books and assignments, I saw an ad for T-shirts for every gender, and there were over sixty different ones, but when you go to order, you can only order a man's shirt or a woman's shirt. I say, your honor, the defense rests.

The best way to poke holes in an agenda is by stating the obvious.

They scared my daughter and made her cry. They punished Patience because she didn't choose what they wanted or believed what they wanted her to believe.

They absolutely believed that they could get away with indoctrination. They were wrong to lie to parents about what they were teaching. It wasn't a matter of right or left politics. It was about right and wrong—and they were wrong.

If they could do that to my kids, they could do that to every kid.

I wasn't going to stand for it. After God, protecting my family is my top priority.

That's how I got into politics.

CHAPTER 4

═══════════════════════════════════

VEGAS

"Are you a climber, a camper, or a quitter? The person at the top of the mountain didn't fall there. Everything that you've gone through is a down payment on your future."
—Bishop Ron Archer

We thought it was just a blue politics, California thing. Paul's airline duties took him from San Ramon, California, to bluer politics Seattle, Washington, back to California again. We lived in the Bay Area and Laguna Niguel before settling into Huntington Beach—in Orange County, California—supposedly the Republican Party stronghold of California.

In Laguna, the problem was bullying. Patience had severe grass allergies, and she'd come home crying with hives on her scalp because kids thought it was funny to rub grass in her hair. Even in kindergarten, Major would come home roughed up or with a black eye. He came home one day and said, "Mrs. Walker said you have blackface!" The school's answer to every problem and issue we raised was that we all just need to hold hands and sing "Kumbaya". They had no actual solution for the bullying and the school's constant response was, "Oh, well a lot of kids in class don't speak English. We have to be more accepting of other cultures. And no one was really hurt. You must understand, it was all just miscommunication."

"No. I don't have to understand. It is bullying! Let me get this straight. Punching my preschool-age son or spitefully rubbing grass in my daughter's hair because the kids in your school think it's funny to trigger an allergic reaction is 'just a misunderstanding,' but accidentally bringing in a snack with peanuts is grounds for suspension? No. You will hold the children responsible for hurting my daughter and son." And school officials did not like that.

It was my first exposure to the problem in our overcrowded schools caused by people illegally crossing our border. Schools have never had enough resources, but now with ballooning class sizes, we are turning a blind eye to the real problems of illegal immigrants oversaturating our communities. There simply aren't enough resources to keep doing everything using American taxpayer funding, trying to do more with less. The reality is we're doing less with less. It's a disservice to our students, and it gets worse every day. This is the Achilles's Heel of socialist doctrines: eventually you will run out of other people's money.

So I held them accountable to their own school rules, and suddenly Patience's progress reflected their dissent of being held to task, with reports saying she can't keep up and her homework and tests are getting marked down. When I confronted her teachers with her work to prove her papers were misgraded, she always got the points back. It was "Oops, there must have been a grading mistake." But there was no mistake. It was adults bullying a child because they didn't enjoy having her mother make them hold all the children to the same standard. They couldn't directly control me, and their frustration was palpable. They were caught in the scathing hypocrisy between the rules and their failure to apply them equally.

That was the mentality in California. Everyone seemed to be in on it, but I never once felt like I was in a sea of inclusive support when I was there. I felt like I was a rock of sanity in an ocean of chaos they were diligently working to wear down. I felt hostility around me when I was walking Patience to school. If Paul and I were walking together holding hands, we'd get the dirtiest looks you could imagine. Death stares for a white guy walking with a woman of color in California—the land of tolerance, where everyone is welcome, where you are embraced with open arms . . . unless you are a conservative, in an interracial marriage, don't submit to government overreach, don't yield to ever-changing ideology, love your country, or don't take a knee.

Our babysitter back then was a very sweet lady who happened to be gay. This was a fact I didn't initially know and truly didn't care about. She was an adult, and that was her business. She saw many instances of hate and intolerance directed at me and would say, "That's just the way it is in Cali, honey. You're wearing yourself out struggling against the river. Swim downstream, pick your battles, it'll all work out."

I enrolled Patience and Major in homeschool, and they thrived. I could fill in gaps I saw in their learning and give them the individual help in areas where they had struggled.

But there was still an undercurrent of something that didn't sit right.

Part of it was the outright rejection that Trump was president, and how using his name in California was all the justification people needed for violence. People have allowed their hatred, fanned by the media, to turn them into the very thing they claim to despise. "It wasn't my fault I beat up that sales associate, took those Nikes, and torched downtown. It was because of Trump." And the city leadership didn't just tolerate it—they encouraged it. That was what was so shockingly profound. It wasn't like Trump had just gotten elected. Their perceived wounds weren't even fresh. He'd been president for three years, and California was rioting and looting and burning.

It made no sense.

I told Paul, "Get us the hell out of here."

"But we just got here." He was exasperated, but he was right.

"These people are crazy," I said, pushing the issue without pushing us to the brink of divorce.

"I know, Raven. Let me think about it. Give me some time."

I posted what I was seeing. I chronicled how I was handling things on Facebook, and I continued after we took the kids out of the school next door and started homeschooling so they could finish out the year. Facebook was new to me, and my observations were polarizing to my followers. When I started getting massive comments from trolls with my followers fending them off, I knew I'd struck a chord.

People were paying attention. I never had what you'd call a "flowery style." I call it like I see it, and people were realizing they weren't alone in what was happening around them, but that they'd become blind to it.

That's when the gloves came off, and I started addressing school indoctrination directly. And people started waking up, which is a very different thing than being "woke." People started tuning in to my Facebook, and it became popular. I started venting, and it became a rallying point for people who were too afraid of the consequences of rocking the boat. We shared information and solutions.

"Raven, did you know . . . " And I shared that.

"Raven, I tried that, and when I talked to my son he was so relieved." And I shared that.

"Raven, my daughter had the same teacher, and this happened . . . "

People started working together, and the movement grew.

A common concern was, "We can't make waves, Raven. It was hard to get our kids into this school, and if your kids don't go to a 'good' school . . . the other schools aren't just bad, they're war zones." That was the nightmare for the parents who cared about their kids. If you didn't drink the Kool-Aid and bow to the agenda, you were ostracized, and your kids could wind up in a school that was borderline criminal.

It was about control.

My followers were all going, "Raven, what are you going to do about this? It's terrible."

I had some ideas. One domino fell after the other.

Paul had a solution. We needed access to an airport with lots of flights, good neighborhoods, and reasonable proximity to Los Angeles for work and modeling commitments. We needed a way to fight back without further traumatizing our children.

We were moving to Vegas.

We moved to Las Vegas in August 2019. The road trip for Major was an adventure with snacks and multiple bathroom breaks in the most remote, inaccessible locations in the sweltering dessert. For Patience, the anxiety of being the new kid again, in a new school, in a new state, weighed on her. I knew how she felt. Her mom was a professional new kid, having attended nine different schools before senior year. As much as I wanted to ease her pain, only time and new, better school experiences would do that.

I watched my kids and their teachers like a hawk to make sure there were no repeats of California, but the kids and their parents were mostly nice. Patience and Major made new friends, and after a month, they'd settled in. No major red flags, and I dove back into work.

Patience was even more of a celebrity in Vegas than she was in California. Her leaving class early to fly to LA for filming caused a school-wide sensation. I once had her on FaceTime while she was in LA, and

I was picking up Major after school. Her teacher noticed us and came to congratulate Patience. Within seconds, three-quarters of the exiting students had surrounded us and were all clamoring to say something to her. She still had acting commitments and modeling contracts and being on TV wasn't as common there as it was in California. Paul would pick her up from school an hour early, and they'd fly to wherever she was working and usually be back by dinnertime. Patience loves to fly. It's in her DNA. As a mother, I was truly impressed with her emerging work ethic. I enforced that school is the priority. If her grades began to suffer, the TV work was done. Her assignments were always on time, and she remained at the top of her class.

A few months later, minor issues popped up again at school, but as I solved and posted about them and shared stories and solutions, more parents got involved and my following grew. People felt I was making a difference in the community, and I enjoyed helping.

I had a long history with Vegas. My media company was flourishing. We signed big names, and I had routinely traveled to Vegas for filming and project meetings. A few years earlier, I was putting together the biggest business deal of my life, and I wound up in the middle of a real life massacre.

In 2007, Paul and I lived in a small condo in the San Francisco area. It was close to the airport, and it allowed us to look after his aging parents. I had founded a company called Race2theRaven. It was a unique, celebrity-themed scavenger event inspired by *The Amazing Race* show, but on steroids. It all started when I asked Paul what he wanted for his birthday. I wanted to do something special for him.

He told me, "We aren't big on birthdays in my family. Don't spend any money."

I told him, "Boy! You don't understand women at all. Anyway, you're marrying a big birthday person. Holidays are for everyone, but your birthday is the day God decided there should be one of you in the world."

I got him a GPS receiver for his car, which is ancient technology now, but back then it was a very cool accessory for his 1998 Camaro. But it wasn't enough. I had caught just one episode of *The Amazing Race*, and it inspired a scavenger-style hunt, which I had done before, but never on an interstate scale.

The first race had a *Superman* theme. (I had nicknamed Paul Superman because he flies. I also call him Angel because he has wings. Fun fact: whatever car Paul is riding in becomes Angel One.) The race had participants finding places that followed Superman's life, picking up items and clues that lead to an amazing climax with plot twists, drama, and indoor skydiving so they could fly. Friends helped, and where I couldn't get volunteers, I hired actors. I made his birthday an experience instead of just a day.

The participants loved it. "You're doing this again next year, right?"

I hadn't thought about it. So I did; and every year, it grew. And every year, I pushed the envelope of possibilities with the ultimate goal of giving everyone something they hadn't experienced before.

Soon it blew up into a multicity, sometimes national, event that had famous pilots, astronauts, and celebrities you've probably seen on television—and a waitlist began to join the Race2theRaven. Part of the mystique was participants never knew where they would ultimately wind up; they would figure it out after the many surprises of living and creating the adventure.

One year, we did a Race2theRaven *Top Gun*-inspired event. Participants were given call signs and given the full "military aviator experience." I was able to get permission from the United States Navy to host part of the event at the Naval Aviation Warfighting Development Center (NAWDC), the real TopGun® academy. It was not an easy feat, but nothing participants had seen in the theatres could compare to breathing the air and feeling the sacred ground of TopGun® beneath their feet. I am forever grateful to the United States Navy for an unprecedented opportunity to show off the dedication and skill of their elite aviators.

I even kept Paul in the dark—which is not an easy task. He had no advantage or knowledge of what to expect. He is a thorough and meticulous person who likes to preplan everything. I would leave fake flight schedules and country searches on my computer and throw misleading clues in the trash bin to ensure he wasn't snooping.

Every year was bigger, in different cities, and with a fresh theme.

Before I knew it, we had film crews following the event, and we were pitching it as a new reality TV show. For our ten-year anniversary race in 2017, we pulled out all the stops and organized a weekend long, *CSI-*

style murder mystery, that also acted as a race-against-the-clock detective story in and around the coolest locations and best events in Las Vegas.

It had grown so large that I needed sponsors and was in negotiations with MGM Resorts to organize races and special events for their select VIPs. It had taken me two years to reach that point. I was excited about it, they were excited about it, and we had a meeting to dry run the event concept and show the MGM execs a proof of concept before they signed the contract. We started rolling out events in January. It was a big deal. There were a million moving parts, and it was going to be Paul's best birthday ever.

Typically, I plan the next race a month after the last one, and the closer we get to showtime, the more time I spend on-site. At that time, we were still living in California, so I was gone a lot. I'd been working almost every week in Vegas since September, organizing and solidifying the plan. If I had a spare second, I was house hunting in preparation for our move to Vegas. The best plans require the best people in key positions to execute so seamlessly that onlookers think magic happened. The very best plans require backups and contingencies because nothing ever completely goes to plan.

I called the event "CS-Eye" because I didn't want to get into a property rights issue with the television show. There were many unique elements to distinguish my event. I did a ton of research to make the experience as real as possible. I loved the criminal justice aspect of the event because criminal justice was my minor in college, and I wanted my husband and clients to have a unique experience investigating different crime scenes. To bring the experience to life, I discovered that the gentleman a *CSI* character was based on still worked in town at the local university. Let's call him Frank.

I reached out early in March when I had three-quarters of the concept set. He thought my idea was groundbreaking, and I hired him as a consultant to make the event as realistic as possible. He was a real retired Las Vegas forensic-CSI specialist. He had great contacts within the police department, other first responders, and forensic labs, and he could bring in actual real-life CSI professionals to make the event feel dynamic, real, and true.

At first, we did most of our work over the phone, and progress was good. I had the framework ready, and Frank filled in the gaps. We had judges, a simulated crime that cut through historic locations, and hard-to-book Vegas events. We established the event logistics and scheduled teams of off-duty law enforcement officers. I had shoulder mics for them and the participants, and I rented black SUVs. We even had CS-Eye vests and badges the state ordered for us. It was the real deal.

The problem, however, was that Frank was a big, fat, married pervert who started our first in-person conversation by asking where my husband was and about the color of my underwear.

I don't have adequate words to describe the frustration that comes from months of research, planning, and money being invested into a business proposal only to be dismissed by some jack tool who wants to feel powerful by holding the "promised land" over you. They don't care if you have a family to feed, how hard you have worked, or if— heaven forbid—your wedding vows are sacred to you. This pay-to-play tactic has never, and will never, work with me. Many people know I had amazing in-laws. What most people don't is that I was the last one to hear my dying mother-in-law's voice. She had been battling an aggressive cancer. Unbeknownst to us, she went off her chemotherapy to be well enough to attend our wedding. She tried to resume her treatments, but she declined very quickly. Then she had a stroke, which impaired her speech. She was struggling to speak, and there was nothing more the doctors could do. Her struggle to speak was excruciating for me, and I felt helpless. "Mom," I said, "I don't know what you're trying to tell me, and I'm scared. I promise you that I will look after Dad, and I will be the wife Paul deserves. I will make sure that Patience grows up to be a lady. I'll make sure the yard is kept, and that Dad takes his medicine and sees the doctor. I won't do it as well as you did, but I'll work every day to be worthy of the faith you've put in me. I love you." She stopped struggling and choked out, "Love you," then died.

Paul's father died five years later from an aggressive cancer that invaded his jaw and ultimately took his ability to speak before it took his life. The last words he was able to speak were strained: "Happy birthday. Love you." I am so grateful, and I owe them so much. I will keep my promise.

Things went downhill after Frank. I established clear working rules, but he and I were never on good terms after that. In fact, the only reason I let him stay was because he threatened to derail the entire event and smear me to the team of law enforcement professionals we'd lined up for the event.

Shortly after that, I learned that he was hitting on my assistant. He was relentless, and he wouldn't take no for an answer, despite having her boyfriend on the set. She quit and fled the set in tears.

She called me later and showed me screenshots of inappropriate messages and requests Frank had sent her. This included messages asking her to audition, pose, and to meet him to "run through" the event. None of these things were known to or sanctioned by myself or our team. I was livid. Having my assistant say she didn't feel safe on my event was a real low point, not only as her boss but also as a Christian and a woman. I was crushed.

She left town, and when I finally found Frank to confront him, he had already pulled all his support, and was well in to bad-mouthing my CS-Eye event to anyone who would listen, while taking credit for the idea, the funding, *everything*. He said it would be a terrible event without him. None of which was true, but it was quite a blow.

That was September. The remains of my crew and I scrambled to refill positions and keep the event on track. Tickets were sold out, and the show had to go on.

The dean of a leading criminal justice university came out with his faculty to see what we were doing and to review our scenarios for the event. They were so impressed they hired us as consultants and have since changed their entire program based on my race. That was a silver lining. We tried to get credited for inspiring the curriculum change, only to find that Frank had somehow already been credited for the concept and the university's position was, "Any dispute was between us and him." History repeating. Once again, my idea, creativity, and hard work were stolen. I consulted my attorney, a good man who informed me that my case was open-and-shut, but the legal fees would likely go into the tens of thousands of dollars. So I win, but I lose.

I made a decision to trust God and be the better person and move on. The truth always comes out. I hunted Frank down; he fled in a rusty minivan with a CSI decal on the side and emailed me, "Nobody's gonna believe you. I have a name. I have a reputation. I have all of law enforcement on my side. And with one call from me, I can make your life and your family's life miserable. You got nothing." The big old perv didn't even have the stones to tell me face-to-face.

It was a hard pill to swallow. I busted my hump and invested my family's money to make the event a success, only to be slandered and ripped off by a married pervert I despised.

I was finally back on track for the CS-Eye race, and my big meeting with the MGM brass and Vegas leadership was just days away. I forwarded Frank's email to lawyers more suited to those battles.

MGM properties are resorts that cater to comfort, relaxation, and pleasure that are only in key locations. That's only the front of the house, and you can Google the rest of their locations and offerings. The behind-the-scenes management was a tougher nut to crack.

I started by asking the concierge at an MGM property. She researched it and finally said, "I can't find the corporate office details. We don't even have their number." And a concierge can get you anything. The barriers to meeting their C-suite folks were no joke, and it took me forever, but I got a meeting in May 2017. I flew in an impressive group to give testimony about the event that included political figures from the cities we'd held the events in, celebrities, and participants that wanted more. We had slick videos of pilots giving our mission briefings with video cuts from our *Top Gun*-inspired race. We ended the pitch with a video of astronaut Christopher Ferguson saying, "I've been in space and never experienced anything like what Raven has created. She is the real deal." The pitch ended in silence. No applause, no questions, just a long, uncomfortable pause.

Then the bigwigs chattered like kids on a field trip, and MGM's Director of Corporate Entertainment Marketing and Sponsorships said, "Great, here's what we're gonna do: make these things happen, and I think we can give you a go." That was May. It was a big task list. By September we were ready.

MGM sponsored the Harvest Festival, and I would be in Vegas for the last week of September. I locked in our meeting for Monday, October 2, to sign what would likely be a six-to-seven figure MGM entertainment deal. They'd pay me to organize and execute each race. They would charge per spot with their higher-end clients, and each race would be a once-in-a-lifetime opportunity with the video to prove it. It was a huge win. I was packaging exciting events I loved to do it with themes like *Top Gun* or *National Treasure*, where I still have invisible ink all over my house from writing clues on the back of Declaration of Independence copies.

I drove in a few days before the meeting and rented a lavish ballroom for the VIP pre-meetings and signing at the Aria. We couldn't get a babysitter in time, and Paul needed to work and stay with the kids. It was the first trip to Vegas without him or my family.

I had a bad feeling when I passed the WELCOME TO FABULOUS LAS VEGAS sign and entered the Strip, but I pushed aside the jitters. I was a hundred meetings, calls, and confirmations away from the biggest deal of my life, but I couldn't shake the feeling that something was off.

I got my room at the Aria and went straight for the ballroom. The art and furnishings were beautiful, and they'd already laid out the bar and equipment for the buffet and a massive wooden conference table with chairs that looked straight out of a palace.

Giant, state-of-the-art display screens surrounded the table, crystal chandeliers hung over it, and elaborate bronze pendant lights and sconces illuminated sitting areas and food-and-drink spaces. They would have been beautiful and nuanced if the lights weren't wildly flickering. The screens were covered in frozen images and dancing static, and it looked like someone had thrown up all over a very expensive Persian rug.

The front desk sent a wave of people to swap out the rugs and clean, and a technician shut off the monitors, but he couldn't exorcise the demons from the machines or the lights; I had a beautiful, expensive dumpster fire still out of control and flickering, with the mayor due in any minute.

Fortunately, I had printed handouts, good window light, and tasty snacks. We had a productive meeting at a coffee table between comfortable couches. We'd confirm the last details on Sunday, in the last working meeting before the MGM signing. When the mayor and her aides left, the staff got back to work, but even after cleaning the room three times and setting up brand new monitors and computers, something was still jinky, and nothing worked right for long.

They were the subtle signs of something not meant to be, but I wasn't going to let that stop me.

I touched base with MGM on Friday. Their director was deeply involved in the weekend Harvest Festival. I asked, "Is there anything

I can do?" I wanted to help if I could. I didn't want to be, "Give me a million dollars, but I won't take time out to support your events." My parents instilled in me a military one-team, one-fight approach to teamwork, and I wanted a relationship with MGM, not just a deal. "I'm happy to help anyway I can."

"I appreciate that," she said, "but it's already in motion. It's packed and sold out, but something always frees up. If you can come by, do. It's a grand event, and if you get the chance, we'll find a seat for you at the festivities. Otherwise, I'll see you Monday."

The weekend was a blur. There were meetings in my room with the team assisting me with coordinating the event until the pizza boxes started stacking up. More meetings in the ballroom with city and police officials. The leads of each section were responsible for the logistics and story to confirm how th event would play out along with its impact on the city in order to make the CS-Eye race a success. Our last meeting was on Sunday. It started at 3:00 p.m.

We set up for it early, but the poltergeists were back, bedeviling the ballroom, and the laptops plugged into the conference table started dying because the power had cut out. The projector screens wouldn't lower, the audio visual didn't work, and all technicians were busy and unable to trouble shoot.

I'm thinking to myself, *Okay, now I need an old priest and a young priest to exorcise the demons and a refund for the ballroom because nothing works*, but I pressed on. Normally it would have been a two-hour meeting, but our presentation was mostly video, and our project planning was computer intensive. Without audio visual, we were struggling.

By 5:00 p.m., we had a spiderweb of extension cords and enough big displays working to seat the extended team and attendees like nothing had happened. The mayor arrived late, with assistants and security, and stayed long enough for the event walkthrough of the crime, locations, and sets. We needed to ensure that our event didn't interfere with law enforcement's daily operations. We had four teams of participants with staggered starts that began at the Desert Motel crime story, and their investigation would lead them through other events happening across Vegas. We ended with the actors performing a turning point in the story, complete with a (simulated) dead victim and gunfight. It went off without a hitch; the mayor okayed the event and was the first to leave. I picked up the phone to order food for the rest of my team that remained, but the phone was dead; by the time I got through on my cell to order, almost everyone else was ready to head out for other plans.

We wrapped at 7:30 p.m. I was so ready for Monday.

I was leaving to have it out with the hotel manager about paying a grand-a-day for a conference room that didn't work when I noticed Detective Nathaniel, Nate, and Johnson still there. He was one of the CSI folks we hired for the event. Paul and I had met him, his wife, and his middle school-aged son in a restaurant when I was rebuilding my crew in the aftermath of Hurricane Frank. He also worked in forensics, and they both seemed passionate about their work. Their dynamic was a little weird, but I needed expertise for the event and, even in a town like Vegas, it was a small pool to pull from. Two things stood out about that initial meeting: the first being that Detective Nate's wife was equally accomplished in law enforcement, and second was that their son was flipping through real autopsy photos while we ate dinner until I asked him to put them away, and neither of them seemed to care.

"What's up, Nate? You look like you've got something to say."

"You probably don't know it, but this hotel's got the best mirrors in the ceiling."

I looked at him like he was crazy. "What?" And I thought the day couldn't get worse. I zipped up my laptop bag and made my way for the door. But for a detective, he didn't get the clue.

"Where's the bedroom in here?"

"There isn't one," I said in my sharpest tone. "How are Patty and your son doing?" I gathered speed, heading out of the room.

"They're at a movie. Wanna go get a drink or something to eat?"

"No, thanks. I still have stuff to do."

"It'll be fun. Or we can just go back to your room."

It thoroughly pissed me off that he couldn't take no for an answer. That nothing in the room worked. That we were still having this conversation. "You really need to go."

"Really?"

"Seriously, dude. I wouldn't touch you to scratch you. There's no way I'd cheat on my husband."

He laughed and dismissed my rejections. I had to grab my things and walk out of the room to get him to leave, and even then he insisted on walking me down to the VIP office to make sure I wasn't lying about wanting to address the technical problems with hotel management. He was surprised when I stopped at security. "Seriously?"

"Yeah, Nate. There's no fricking way in hell. Go find your wife. Think about pulling this shit ever again, and you're not only fired from the event but I'll also call your captain at the station."

"Fine." Detective Nate stuffed his hands in his pockets and stomped away like a toddler.

"Do I need to escort him out?"

I looked up and kept looking up. The security guard was one big, tall, buff dude. "Thanks, but no. He won't be back."

He nodded approvingly but followed him out anyway.

After I got my refund and a comp from the hotel manager for all the problems, I finally made it back to my room. There was still a broken-down pizza-box wall. Nobody had cleaned.

It's the little things that build up in people that make us explode.

Through all the day's frustrations, I forgot to pick up souvenirs for the kids. It's a stupid tradition, but my mother did it faithfully with me. Whenever she travelled, she always brought me a memento. A T-shirt, a key chain, whatever. I went down to the lobby of the hotel, but it was closed. I knew things would be open on the Strip, but I felt uncomfortable strolling down the Las Vegas Strip at night alone.

I weighed what we'd accomplished against all the obstacles and annoyances and decided that even though it was a Sunday night, and the lobby shop was closed, I was going to find souvenirs to bring back to my kids. I wasn't going to let this incredibly stressful trip end empty-handed, and I missed them terribly. Then I found the Aria manager, and he dispatched a maid to my room before I even got all the words out, promising all would be made right.

We'll see.

I left the Aria lobby after 9:00 p.m. to look for souvenirs, but not much was open on a Sunday night in Vegas that wasn't serving tequila cocktails in three-foot-tall glasses. I searched one store after the other, and I was in the middle of finding nothing when I got a call from MGM.

"Did I wake you?"

"No. I'm just out looking for stuff for the kids."

"Well, it's winding down a bit. But we have a concert still going on. You might catch a bit of the ambience if you wanted to stop by."

"Okay. How do I find you?"

"Jason Aldean's getting ready to hit the stage. It will be a great show. Tell security you're here to see me. They'll know where I am."

I rushed down the Strip toward Mandalay Bay. A Vegas block feels like the equivalent length of a football field, so normally I would have taken the bus or flagged down a taxi, but I was too excited.

Although I was completely out of breath from the unexpected sprint, I could hear the band playing way before I got there. A canyon of souvenir shops still looked open across from Mandalay Bay. I decided to go there for souvenirs after the festival. I walked through the packed festival. People were chilling and dancing. It was contagious, and it felt good and fun—like a festival should. But I couldn't see how to get into the concert. I couldn't find the gate. There was an opening, and people were shouting, "Come on in." I didn't see security, but the crowd carried me into the chaos of the concert, past the T-shirt stands and beer vendors. By the time I found security, I was tired. Weeks of preparation and battles all weekend had worn me out. I shouted who I was and who I wanted to see over the song.

"I don't know her," he said, in a deep country accent.

I shouted, "She's in charge of the concert."

"'Kay. Festival's almost over. Once we open the gates, I can find where she is and take you there."

They hadn't even started encores, and it looked like it would be a while.

"Thanks! Don't worry. I'll catch her tomorrow."

The crowd was thinning, and it was almost 10:00 p.m. I had the biggest moment of my professional career in the morning. I truly wasn't up for strolling around Vegas at night without my husband, much less being in the middle of a raging block party. I was ready for bed.

I stopped at the first crosswalk past the festival, banging the button to change the light, and scrolling my phone for MGM in my contacts. I was going to call and leave my congratulations on a great festival and let her know the crowd was so big I couldn't get close to the stage, but that I would see her in the morning.

The light changed. I was halfway across the crosswalk, heading to the canyon gift shop for souvenirs, when I heard firecrackers popping off. I turned to look up. I wasn't alone; the crowd of people all around me searched the sky for fireworks as we crossed. It was a festival. It never dawned on me that there wouldn't be fireworks. But nothing was there. No lights or colors in the sky. Then there were screams.

Blood-curdling screams.

An ambush hit me hard in the back as a heavy, saturated wall of panicking people landed on top of me. Down I went, face-first onto the filthy, unforgiving asphalt. I immediately tried to get to my feet. Another wave of people knocked me over. Hit me again.

Within seconds I was caught in a moving stampede as a silhouetted mob climbed over me in the golden light of Mandalay Bay.

Heavy men in heeled cowboy boots were running over my back. Shoes with metal buckles kicked my head and hips. The weight of all those people was crushing my lungs, hands, and legs.

I went down hard, my purse the only thing that prevented a full face-plant on the sidewalk. I couldn't lift my head from being facedown in my oversized purse, and I became terrified I was going to suffocate. This was a real possibility, but for the grace of God, the contents of my purse spilled out upon impact with the sidewalk, giving me a small air pocket until I could turn my head sideways.

The contents of my purse scattered wider around me as I struggled to get up, only to be knocked even harder to the ground.

Pop. Pop. Pop.

Panicked festivalgoers trampled me. I couldn't get my head off the asphalt. I was afraid my skull and back would crack under their feet and from their weight.

Strings of firecrackers cracked off. Screams and shouts.

I felt like the knotted-up clothes in a spin-cycle washing machine banging and slamming against the floor. My body was cracking, bleeding, and burning.

I couldn't get traction or my bearings. I reached for my license, keys, and the few items from my purse that were closest to me. Heavy people stomped me down. I grabbed my phone and got to my knees, and they crashed into my side, fell on top of me, climbed over me, and didn't look back.

Pop. Pop. Pop.

I was getting kicked and hit from all directions.

Pop. Pop. Pop.

I yelped in pain. The petrol smell of warm asphalt. Their panic. My disoriented panic. I could taste blood in my mouth

Pop. Pop. Pop.

I pushed against the tide. Got to my feet. Stumbled forward with the crowd. My purse strap and phone death-gripped in my hands and held against my chest.

I ran. They ran.

We ran in a pack.

The people and pops became a den of noise in the crazy Vegas light. The screaming never stopped. Never.

People on the street started diving behind cars. Into the souvenir shops. Flattening themselves to the ground around corners. Crouching behind any cover they could find.

People were covering their ears and crying. I don't know if they were bleeding. At that point, I didn't know what I was seeing anymore.

Police car lights flashed as a red-and-blue blur as they raced by.

I ran.

I wanted out of the fray. The pack I was running with thinned. Before I knew it, I was running alone down Las Vegas Boulevard.

I never turned around, and I never looked back. I just wanted to get the hell out of dodge. All I knew was something was wrong. I got caught in a stampede, and I ran and ran and ran. I was panting and out of breath.

I used to always joke about the people in a scary movie. There's always the one who looks back and falls. She gets killed because it gave the bad guy enough time to catch her.

That wouldn't be me.

I didn't stop running until I was back at the entrance of the Aria, face-to-face with a policeman putting up a metal barricade. We stared at each other.

"Ma'am, are you okay?"

"No, I just need to get back to my room."

He frowned, shaking his head. "Ma'am. What I mean is, do you need to go to a hospital?"

"Why would I need to go to a hospital?"

"Ma'am, you're bleeding."

He was serious. My mouth was full of blood and it was running out of the corner of my mouth. I looked down. I was clutching what was left of my purse in crossed arms against my chest and there was a wide, wet stream of blood soaking down the front of my shirt. I didn't realize. It didn't seem like it was me.

"Ma'am, let me send you to the hospital."

"I don't need a hospital. I didn't start the stampede. They broke my phone."

"Were you involved in the incident, ma'am? What's your room number?"

I was full of adrenaline, completely disoriented, and I felt like he was accusing me. "Why do I have to tell you that? I didn't do anything. It wasn't my fault. I'm the one who got ran over." I didn't know what he was talking about. I still wasn't sure what happened.

"It's because of the shooting, ma'am. We have to account for every MGM guest."

"What shooting?"

"The shooting at Mandalay Bay. You're hurt. Maybe in shock. It looks like you may have been there."

"I stopped by the festival. And there was . . . There was . . ." My mind raced, trying to process what all there was.

I gave him my room number. I reiterated I wasn't going to the hospital.

When he was satisfied I wasn't shot, he let me pass.

The front desk clerk shrieked when he saw me. I wanted a first-aid kit, but he backed away from the desk as I stepped up to it and all I could think was, *Dude, can you be anymore pathetic? I'm the one bleeding over here.* What I said was, "You had better not charge me for ruining the towels."

He nodded. I left. Walking through the lobby of the Aria was surreal. I have never seen a Vegas lobby so empty. No people, no noise, no activity. It was silent and creepy. The elevator was white and gold and bright. I was alone in a box that played salsa music. The elevator opened into an empty corridor, and I could see my room.

The door was open. It freaked me out. After everything to get there, I'm like, *Now what?*

The pizza boxes were gone. The lights were off, the TV was on, and the news was playing. I remembered we were watching *Forensic Files* on

CNN during our meeting and due to ongoing technical issues, it was frozen on the TV. The room was choking with industrial-strength Febreze, so the maid must have recently left, and I wasn't going to stand in the hall puzzling through why my door was open, so I pushed my way in, turned on every light, and locked the door. I had had my fill of whodunits for the day.

I went to the sink, washed my face and arms. I was covered in road rash that looked like leprosy. What wasn't bleeding was oozing. My body was raw and in pain. I pressed cold, wet towels against my bleeding wrist while I watched the coverage of the shooting. Blood had soaked through my jeans, dried, and welded them to my legs, so I couldn't take them off. I was grossed out and scared. I ran some bath water to attempt to soak them off. The news crawler read, WORST MASSACRE IN US HISTORY. My blood dripped on to the floor. I used all the towels in the room before the bleeding finally stopped.

I don't replay that memory often, but when I do my mind goes, *Raven, how could you not know you were in the middle of a shooting? Why didn't you take cover?*

And I can't believe I made myself a target, running down the street like a maniac when someone was shooting up the festival. I didn't see the infamous window blown out or the gaping hole where the shooter was stationed. I didn't see any of that. I was too busy getting trampled in the middle of a terrified crowd when fight-or-flight kicked in, and I had no way to fight.

It was hard to get a call out of the hotel. At 12:30 a.m., I finally got through to Paul on my nearly dead, broken cell phone.

"Paul, something happened here, and I'm hurting."

I had woken him up, and he was desperately trying to process my hysterical ranting.

"I'm coming home," I cried.

"Darling, just wait until morning when it's daylight. I don't want you on the road tonight. Do you need to go to a hospital?"

"No, I'm okay."

"I love you. Call me when you're heading out."

"Okay."

"Thank God." I could hear the concern in his voice. But he must have turned on his phone and the TV after I hung up because he called me back almost immediately.

"Darling, *what's* going on over there? I called your phone and the hotel, and I couldn't get through. My pilots going into Vegas are reporting they are landing there in active gunfire. Where are you? You sure you're alright?"

I told him what happened. I wanted to talk to my babies, but I was glad they were asleep and didn't know. "I don't want to be here, Paul. I'm ready to hit the road and come home."

"Whoa! Stop. You've been through a lot. You're safe now. You should get some rest and come back tomorrow."

"I'm fine now. And it is tomorrow." I wasn't even thinking about the MGM thing anymore. I was suppose to ink a seven-figure deal in mere hours, and nothing in me wanted to stay in town. Mandalay Bay is an MGM property. I figured they would have bigger issues come daybreak.

"Raven."

"Paul."

He sighed. Long and loud. "Raven, just think about it. Do what feels right. And call me before you leave."

"Roger that. I love you. I've got another call coming in. I'll talk to you soon."

It was Detective Jay, an amazing officer who saw through Frank's lies and continued to help me with the race.

"Jesus, Raven, what did you do? We were just with you."

"I'm good, Jay."

"Really? It's chaos here, and we're heading to the scene. You really okay?"

"I am. Scraped up and worse for wear, but I'm fine."

"Oh man, I had a feeling you were there. You need a doctor? I can send over a patrolman."

"No, I think I'm okay."

"That's good. Stay safe and get some rest."

Click.

After nearly twenty minutes trying to get through, I reached the front desk. "Pull my car around please. I'm leaving."

She goes. "Sorry, ma'am, we can't. We're on lockdown."

"Lockdown? What does that mean?"

"The officer in the lobby says we have to account for every single person, and that, for now, we need to shelter in place."

"I was there, but I'm okay. I just need to get home."

"Mrs. Harrison, I understand. As soon as they clear us, I'll call you and have your car brought around."

"I understand." I didn't, but I did. "Be safe."

"You too, ma'am."

My room was high up and faced Interstate-15, so I sat at my window, trying to clear my head, watching. I-15 was the major artery on the west side of the Las Vegas Strip and there were no cars, but a police car was running its lights at every cross street to the Mandalay Bay.

I have never seen Vegas so empty.

I was exhausted, but too keyed up to sleep, checking my watch and waiting.

My MGM exec called me just before dawn. "Raven, I'm glad I could reach you. Your cell's out of service. How are you, dear? Are you hurt?"

"I'm banged up, but I'll live. I was just leaving the concert when everything went to hell. Where are you?"

"At the hospital. When the shooting started, a security guard threw himself on me to protect me and dragged me out of the line of fire. Very brave, but he broke his arm and my ankle getting me offstage."

"I'm glad that's the worst of it."

"Yes. It was horrible. It's still terrible. We're working with the police to find out how the hell this happened, and injured are still coming into the hospital. You weren't here, and I wasn't sure if that was good or bad. I remember calling you, but I never saw you."

"I made it to the concert."

"It's a relief to know you made it out."

"I'm glad you did too, but I'm ready to go home."

"You do that. It's too much to process right now. We'll talk later this week. Be careful getting home."

It was a polite way of saying there's obviously not going to be a race meeting because lawyers were about to get unleashed all around.

A couple of cars driving down I-15 caught my eye. It was 5:30 a.m. I was watching the freeway all night and called the front desk again.

A young man answered. "Mrs. Harrison. Good. We just got word. The lockdown's over. Can we bring your car around?"

"Yes." My heart jumped. "I'm heading down now." I frantically stuffed all my things into my bags, and I ran crying all the way to the valet.

My SUV was running. The valet put my luggage in the trunk, started opening the door, and stopped. "Ma'am, you sure you're okay?" In my haste I had opened some wounds and they began to bleed again. I looked where the valet was standing. The blood was pooling where I was standing.

I felt weak, but there was no way I wasn't leaving that second. Then I realized I hadn't changed, and I was a mess. "It was a rough night. Hey, if I just want to get out of here without getting stopped a thousand times asking if I need to go to the hospital, what's the best way?"

He pointed me to Wayne Newton Drive and the back way locals used to get to the freeway. I drove and didn't stop.

I thanked God and prayed for everyone as I drove by police cars, trying not to get pulled over and delay getting home. I just wanted out of Vegas, and I was so happy when I got on I-15 and hit the speed limit. I had 260 miles of gas in my tank, and 220 miles to go.

I didn't stop to eat or drink. It still took too long to get home.

I don't remember showering or changing or even going to bed. It was daylight when I fell asleep and daylight when I woke up. I heard a loud *pop!* and I couldn't breathe. Everything hurt. Every movement made me wince. I felt like I was being stabbed in the lungs.

Paul went pale when he found me. It was late morning, and the kids were already at school. "You need an ambulance?" I shook my head, and that was a mistake.

I could hear him talking to the doctor's office, but between the pain and anxiety, the next thing I remember was Paul opening the door to ease me into the passenger seat.

I froze when I saw it. I would have screamed if I could. We had a BMW X5 SUV with a light-colored leather interior.

On the back of the driver's seat, staring back at me, was the bloody face-and-shoulder imprint of a woman I didn't know. Even Paul gasped.

She must have fallen on me, bleeding when I was struggling to stand in the mob. It was perfectly persevered. I could tell it was a woman. I could see her eyebrows and eyelashes in detail. I don't know how it could have happened after four hours of driving with my back pressed against the seat, but there she was. I could see her expression. She was screaming. It looked like it could have been silk-screened.

"We need to go," Paul said, securing me into the seat. Her face was frightening. I couldn't look away until Paul came back from the house with a towel and threw it over her.

I felt every crack and pebble in the road, and, *"Oh my God, I had somebody's face I didn't know" plastered in blood on my driver's seat, under a beach towel.*

It was a nightmare that wouldn't stop.

The receptionist took one look at me, and the doctor saw us right away. I hadn't seen myself in a mirror since before I left my room at the Aria for Mandalay Bay, and I felt bad for Paul. The way the nurse was scowling at him, my bruises must have been bad. She had that "I know what you did" look directed at Paul.

"Wait, you don't understand," I said to her, and the doctor knocked and walked in.

"What are we in for?" Her chipper demeanor fell away. "Ohhh." She looked at my arms and under my shirt and poked and motioned to the nurse. "We're going to have to strip off these clothes. Sir, you can wait outside."

"No. He stays."

"Okay. You sure? You fall down the stairs? You're covered in contusions, and you have a boot-shaped bruise on your back."

"Stand down." It was hard to talk. "I got caught in a stampede."

"A stampede? Where were you?"

"In Vegas."

"Oh, my gracious. The shooting. Raven, are you shot?"

"I don't think so, but yes, the shooting on the news. Many people are dead. I couldn't stand to stay there. My wrists are shredded. My jaw hurts. Breathing hurts. People ran over me. I couldn't get up, okay? Everything hurts, okay?"

I started crying.

"It's going to be alright." The doctor opened the door and told all available personnel to come in immediately. She turned to the nurse: "She needs a full workup: exams, X-rays, CT scans, and an MRI. Everything. Tell them this is their priority. I'm sending her over now."

When the nurse left, Paul helped me dress.

"I'm also setting you up with post-trauma counseling."

"Let's not get ahead of ourselves, doc. I'll go after you fix everything that hurts."

Fixing me turned out to be a laundry list of pain: spiral fracture in my left arm, two fractured ribs, stitches to make sure my wrist didn't open again, a hairline fracture in my jaw, and multiple contusions that were swollen, yellow, and purple. It took three months for the boot print on my back to fade away. My road rash was infected and weeping.

The body count grew until sixty-one were dead, including the terrorist shooter Stephen Paddock. Hundreds fled to nearby McCarran International Airport to escape, which shut it down. Over 850 people were injured, nearly half of them with gunshot or shrapnel wounds. It was a massacre. Families of victims and the public demanded to know what happened. The FBI, ATF, and Nevada Police investigated and supported the Clark County Sheriff's office. They ran down conspiracy theories and worked out what had happened and how it had happened. They circled around "why," but never answered that question. His motive remains unknown. He shot himself. Despite all the expertise and technology they brought to bear, the dead man told no tales.

Vegas and the nation desperately needed something, and the news picked up social media stories to give us heroes. Some were brave during the shooting. A few protected and saved others. The rest was bullshit. It was a massacre; the herd stampeded and hid where they could. I don't blame them, but I didn't see the heroes. I saw scared men throwing women down to flee. People kicking and climbing over me to get away. The spin made me furious.

Faced with that terror, I wish I could say I saw heroes, but I didn't. I saw scared people, like me. I saw panic and fear.

I watched until I couldn't stand it anymore.

But there were still headlines when I browsed the Internet. Every time I saw a picture of the broken windows at the Mandalay Bay casino where the shooter stood, I didn't feel so good.

The anxiety was overwhelming. My mind continued processing what happened, and I remembered more. My brain still wanted it to be fireworks I just couldn't see, but that's not what it was. I knew I was safe, but the mind does play tricks. I was on the mend, but every time I closed my eyes, I was scared and either fighting to stand in a surge of bodies or running down the street with a target on my back. Waking up, I thanked God I was waking up.

Pain and PTSD. I felt horrible. The doctor prescribed medicine to help, but I only took it once. While it made the pain go away, it gave me hallucinations, and—to add insult to injury—double vision.

I couldn't watch Patience and Major like that. Thank God Paul could come home until I could see straight again. Apparently, I'm sensitive to the best family of meds to kill that kind of pain. My doctor said I had other options to try, but truth be told, I wasn't going to ride the pharmacy roller coaster again after everything I'd been through.

Getting through the first two weeks of multiple fractures and contusions with just ibuprofen was miserable. Once I got through that, I knew I was broken. I asked my doctor during a follow-up, "How could I have driven home this hurt?"

"You were in shock," she said.

"Why do I still feel gross?"

"Your body's healing. Now you have to attend to those scars no one else can see."

I really didn't like the sound of that. I felt I handled things pretty well, considering the circumstances. Watching Patience and Major play with their friends was when it hit me.

I could have died.

I spent two years relentlessly trying to get in front of MGM, showing what I could do, putting together the proposal of a lifetime.

I had been fighting for respect, money, and business.

And I was right there. No one had a concept like Race2theRaven or a way to make it real.

I was going to make history.

Paul said to me, "Aren't you glad that you didn't sign the deal? All the lawyers coming after MGM would be after you."

Lawyers sue everyone they can. It's how they're wired. Someone has to pay them to make sure, "You may be entitled to compensation."

But if I'm being honest, I wasn't glad. Not at all. I wanted what I had worked so hard for. I earned that deal. But the reason it didn't happen was more agonizing than losing the deal itself.

I focused on my recovery, other ventures, the endless battle of trying to make America great again for my kids, and resolving and sharing the solutions to issues in our country.

How does this happen? I did everything I was supposed to do. My conversations with God were frantic.

I had done it. Built successful businesses. I was a successful wife to a great and loving man. We were partners who made a family together with two wonderful children. It was physical, tangible proof of what I could do, and the talent God had bestowed on me. Why was losing one deal such a hard fall?

It took me a while to understand. It wasn't just the aching disappointment of being so close to what I had dreamed the next part of my life would be—only to have it taken away—but also the lack of direction of what was next.

That was my gift, right? That was my calling, wasn't it? To wear the mantle of motherhood and family and to nurture them and my businesses. That was the place I had made for myself in the world.

I underestimated the pain and how long it would take my body to recover, but the worst part was the nightmares. I couldn't seem to shake them.

We had a lot invested in the MGM demo, and because I was healing, there was much I couldn't do, and I was miserable. I pushed myself hard. Probably too hard. But I was a survivor. I could figure anything out, and so I pushed myself harder. I was angry and everything hurt.

I pushed through it until I could do the things I needed to do and be who I needed to be again. But I felt like I was only going through the motions. Something was missing. Something was still wrong.

The nightmares didn't let up. I finally figured out that it wasn't just the fear and pain of what happened and didn't happen in Vegas that was magnified in my dreams, it was something more fundamental. Good people died in that massacre. I survived; so many others didn't. I was glad I lived and, somehow, I felt guilty. I had confronted my mortality. I looked at my children. I had so much to lose and so much I wanted to give, it frightened me. What would happen if I wasn't there? What would happen to the ones I loved?

I ran through the middle of a killing field with a target on my back, and I didn't even know it. I grew up on military bases; I know what gunfire sounds like. Even when I was searching for fireworks, on some level, I knew something was wrong, and it added to my guilt for not recognizing it. For not being as smart as I think I am. For not immediately assessing what was happening around me. But to me, gunfire was synonymous with the war for freedom, the weapons I watched the government take away from people in Berlin, and how patriots on base trained to fight for it so we could be safe. I had no context for the assault at a festival in Las Vegas, Nevada, USA.

Could I have done something? Anything?

At that moment, no. I was overrun and crushed and lived, wondering, *Why me?*

Why was I saved?

I realized two things: my gift to inspire wasn't the extent of my gift. It was a God-given talent I was supposed to grow, and I knew I would never get over the shooting and everything that had happened—unless I went back to Vegas and the Mandalay Bay to confront my fear. I learned from my parents as a military brat that you don't negotiate with terrorists. I couldn't stop or stay away. I wouldn't let the terrorist win. When you succumb to the fear, they win.

As if on cue, lawyers started calling. "You were injured. It was the MGM Mandalay Bay's fault. We want to represent you. You may be entitled to compensation." It made me sick. I lived. I had good insurance. There were people far worse off. A friend of mine was shot through the jaw, and she was in awful pain. I gave them her number. Her jaw was wired shut, she was having a rough time, and there was nothing I could do but answer her texts as soon as they came in.

But the lawyers kept calling. Paul asked if joining a lawsuit would help me get closure and help me heal. It was a fair question, but it wouldn't. I lived. I knew what I had to do. I wasn't going to sue MGM, and I didn't want to be a part of any lawsuit. Let that money go to those people who lost what can't be replaced. I felt that way then. I feel that way now.

===

We did the CS-Eye race the following January, and I was with the Las Vegas Metropolitan Police Department and CSI again. I was with them literally two hours before the shooting, and we were together again for the event. I knew them. They knew me. Everyone shared their stories and tragedy, but we all needed to move on. We needed to show Vegas was resilient, and we did. Vegas Strong. We sent a signal to the world.

I had to go to Vegas again. After I retraced my steps, I kept going back. Soon we moved and had a house in Vegas and my kids were in school there.

You don't let the fear win. It's an actual fight. A constant battle. One that's hard for others to see. But if you let fear win, your life will never be yours to live.

The next year, we held another race. It was James Bond-themed; we called it "Casino Royale, RI6" (Raven Intelligence 6).On the sixty-fourth floor of Mandalay Bay Resort, there's a lounge called Skyfall.

I probably spent a good hour at the foot of Mandalay Bay trying to breathe and get the courage to walk in and go up to that restaurant. It was the hardest I've ever battled any kind of PTSD. My feet were glued to the lobby floor. Paralyzed with fear. My heart about to explode.

I couldn't let my fear have that win.

I looked down at my feet.

Raven, you're better than this.

No, I'm not. Go. Get out.

I looked at the corridor past the lobby that leads to the Delano part of the resort.

It's too far. I can't do it.

Then just one step.

One step? . . . I can do one step.

Okay. One. Just one.

It took me an hour to get to the elevator.

It's not the thirty-second floor of Mandalay Bay. It's the sixty-fourth floor, in a different building in the resort.

It's gold, like Mandalay Bay.

Yes, it is.

One step at a time.

Another hour later, I was in the Skyfall lounge.

CHAPTER 5

CALL . . . OR CALLING

"The mantle of leadership is not the cloak of comfort,
but rather the robe of responsibility."
—Thomas S. Monson[1]

It took more than a year before I stopped shuddering when I saw Mandalay Bay, but I don't cringe anymore driving down the Strip. By this time we had moved to Vegas from California. Living in Vegas meant feeling a lot of things. I came to Vegas feeling like I was born under a dark cloud. I left Vegas finally, and clearly, understanding my calling, but I was busy and unsure.

Learning and doing were my tickets to what I wanted: survival, independence, my family, my businesses. I learned from my mistakes, applied what I learned, and worked hard until I was a better me. Wash, rinse, repeat. My mother taught me as a little girl that my education could take me places, and that the more I learned and the better I did would give me bigger opportunities and open more doors.

Growing up, that meant school and college. Schools are as critical today as they were then. As a mother wanting the same opportunities for my children, it's become all too clear to me that an ideological occupation has widely replaced history and real civics. The intellectual fascism of "you will do and believe what I say" has replaced teaching critical thinking in kindergarten through twelfth grade and college education. Our youth are now socially, not academically, primed. Boys are taught that they are, or can, be girls, and girls are taught they are, or can, be boys—or any fluid-something in between. This is a lie, and a recent assault that "educators" disguise as inclusion, but it's not. It's an agenda that's crept into even elementary school classrooms, sometimes overtly, often as part of the shadow curriculum schools don't want parents to know about. I've seen it to varying degrees at every school my children have attended. It's important to remember that for hundreds of thousands of years, the human race has grown and evolved because of the men and women who made families and had children. We shouldn't need to assure our children that being a man or a boy, or a woman or a girl, is a real thing and that it's okay.

Inclusivity is a good thing, and bullying and hurting others should never be tolerated in school or anywhere for any reason. It's true that we have the right to believe what we do, and no one has the right to take our beliefs and values away for fear of hurting someone's feelings. Sex and gender are not fashion. I respect an adult's right to think, feel, and live as they believe under the law, but I will never accept these ideas being forced on children. Respect is a two-way street. As of late, there is a dangerous ideology that demands we accept another's values at the expense of our own. The irony being that I am fighting for their freedom to disagree with me.

Our children are also increasingly taught that their value and potential resides in the color of their skin and that, based on how much melanin they produce, they are likely to be bad or good, an oppressor or victim, a success or failure because of the actions of someone else. It's an agenda buried in critical race theory, activist history, and far-left teacher agendas.

Everyone is born with different strengths, challenges, advantages, and disadvantages. A black man, Barack Obama, was elected to the highest office in the nation—*twice*, and mostly by white voters. If there was real systemic racism in the United States today, that would not have been possible. So, if you believe that systemic racism is prevalent in the US, at the highest levels, how did his election happen? Either there is no systemic racism, or President Obama was complicit in that racism, and that is ridiculous. Whether you agree or disagree with his policies—and I disagree with every single one of them and did not vote for him either time—his election was a great and historic event in America, a clear indicator of just how far we've come as a nation. I want my children and every child in America to believe they can be president, or a fireman, or a doctor, or a policeman, or whatever they dream to do one day. Not everyone will get there, but there are other brilliant futures for them to find along the way.

President Reagan once said, "If fascism ever comes to America, it will come in the name of liberalism."[2] Concrete definitions aren't popular anymore, but Merriam-Webster defines fascism as: "a political philosophy, movement, or regime . . . that exalts nation and often race above the individual and that stands for a centralized autocratic government. . . ."[3] Throw in a toxic dose of Marxism and socialism, and that's exactly where we are today. I was fighting it in the schools and local government, mostly for my kids, when I got the call.

It was 8:00 p.m. on a Saturday and my cell phone rang. I didn't recognize the voice. The call was clear, but he sounded far away. "Hello, Raven Harrison." It was the chairman of the Republican Party of a strong republican state. "I hope it's not too late to talk."

"No. It's fine." If you could have seen my face, you'd know how confused I was by the call. It came out of the blue, and I was talking to one of the most influential men in politics and an important person in the Republican Party.

My first thought was, *Now, what did I do?* "What can I do for you, sir?"

"Really? It's what I can do for you. I got your name from a congressional candidate I admire."

"Well, sir, that was nice of him. He gave you my name for what?"

"I wrote down what he said, and I quote, 'Raven is the conservative who is going to change this party forever. You need to have her on your side or get out of her way.' So I suppose I'm calling to get you on our side."

I didn't know what to say. I was trying to take notes, but that made me drop my pencil. To say it was an awkward pause would be an understatement.

"Hello? You still there?"

I should have said, "Thank you," or, "That was kind of him," but what came out of my mouth was . . . an utterly baffled, "He told you I was a greasy politician?"

Then there was a pause on his end and what sounded like a snicker. "I'm going to pretend you didn't say that and tell you this: we're going to be censoring a senator who voted to convict President Trump in his second impeachment trial."

"What does that have to do with me?"

"Have you ever considered running for office?"

"No. Not ever." But I was heavy into current politics and saw where it was going wrong.

"I'd like you to consider it. I realize you don't live here now, but you could if you wanted to."

My heart was pounding. Be polite. Don't burn a bridge. "Sir, I'm extremely flattered." I just wanted to get off the phone. "It's a big decision. Do you mind if I think it over?"

"Absolutely, but don't take too long. Your country needs you."

I set the phone down and looked at Paul. It was movie night, the kids were asleep, and his head was in my lap. "Isn't that the most absurd thing you ever heard?" I expected him to laugh and say something like, "That was wild," or, "That could only happen to you," but he didn't. He had an intense look on his face.

"Darling," he said, "honestly, I think God put you on earth to do this."

I was floored. "So this is how people see me? Crooked? Like a politician? Like I'm a liar?"

"No," he said, holding my hands. "It just makes so much sense. The fire. The fight. Your resourcefulness." Then he did laugh. "I kinda feel like we should have seen this coming."

"Whoa." We were in the middle of COVID-19. Every week was a different lockdown, and every week the schools changed their rules, procedures, and controls. Between online and part-time school and isolation, the kids were in very different places. For Major, it was an opportunity to watch more shows and game with his friends online; school was mostly a checklist he had to get through to get to the fun stuff. For Patience, it was absolute misery. She enjoyed going to school and missed her friends and the freedom to go where she wanted. She hated being stuck at home. People were scared and frustrated. The media filled every channel and web search with fearmongering and half-truths and manufactured divisions. Everyone had had enough of the pandemic, the lockdowns, and lies.

I was still thinking about the call. I wanted to do something. I could make things better. Was that really my calling?

A soldier comes to know quickly if they were born to be a soldier. It's a fire in you. It's that passion that not everybody can understand that's your calling. It's a togetherness of understanding what you can do and what you will do. It's who you are. No one runs into a burning building or puts themselves in harm's way to save someone else, or lays down their life, for the free college.

There are two hallmarks in a Christian's life: the day you get saved and the day you find out why. A calling happens in that moment, just you and God at the crossroads of what we are meant to be, and what you choose to be. When they align, you know. Until that point, I always felt like I was a puzzle that was almost together, but not quite done, and God is the ultimate puzzle maker. Our callings are bigger than us. That's when I realized that my duty was bigger than my business and even bigger than Patience and Major or me and Paul. It was a staggering realization. I would still raise them to adulthood as happy as I could make them, with the right tools for life, and someday see them walk down the aisle.

I also felt something big was on the horizon, affecting us all. The next Sunday, I went to church. I said, "God, wow. Thanks. You're not very subtle." But I didn't ask for subtle. I wasn't made for subtle. I needed to fight, to make the world around me right, to do whatever God was telling me to do.

Paul asked me what I wanted to do about the call. He was looking at different jobs and flights he could take to allow him to commute to work and said it was up to me.

I was ready to answer the call. But it wasn't what anyone wanted or expected. I'm joining this fight, but I can't do it here where the kids are locked up and masked up. I have to go somewhere I know.

"I think I need to go home." I was always on the move, but in between, I stayed with my grandma in a small town where she tried hard to raise me to be a good southern lady.

I'm not entirely sure that this is what she envisioned, or maybe it was.

"Home?" asked Paul. "You grew up all over the place. Where?"

My heart knew. It was where I was born. Where I spent my summers, holidays, and breaks. Where most of my family lived. Where my best childhood memories were made. It was the only constant in my chaotic life.

Texas.

CHAPTER 6

===============================

TEXAS

"Pray as though everything depended on God.
Work as though everything depended on you."
—Saint Augustine[1]

It was a homecoming decades in the making. Texas fit like broken-in jeans, and I had a story for every little worn spot and tear. My best memories of home and my grandmother, Exa Dale Sandling, are in Baytown. It wasn't perfect—nowhere is; but it was a mostly calm eye-in-the-storm that was my life.

Oil, or "Texas Tea," is the lifeblood of Baytown and Texas. When the wind blows in from the West, you can smell the rotten-egg kerosene of the refineries. Usually it's just a whiff, but the pungent fumes can make your eyes water. Interstate-10 roughly divides Baytown into haves and have-nots. East of the interstate was growing and prospering; West of the interstate was not. My grandmother lived at 600 Lloyd Dr. in a modest three-bedroom brick house on a corner lot. It was the central hub and gathering place of our family. The oil industry brought an influx of immigration to Baytown, along with cycles of growth and decay. With oil money also came opportunity . . . if you had the determination to take it.

Baytown was small-town America where everyone knew everyone—especially our family. There was primarily one of everything: one barber, one auto repair, one plumber, etc. Except churches. Like many places in the South, churches dotted the landscape. I was raised Catholic, but my Texas family are all Baptist. Catholic church service was one hour on Sundays, and we never missed a Sunday. In the Southern Baptist churches, service went from Sunday to Wednesday. It was mandatory, long, loud, and overwhelming for me at times. It was like night and day from the serene, structured, very monotone service I was used to. Having my cousins with me at my grandmother's church really helped me adapt to the stark contrast.

My mom was a hometown celebrity, in a way that only a small town could produce, and a reporter interviewed her every time we went to Grandma's house. My mother was a tall, statuesque, Native American beauty with hip-length hair. The local newspaper was the *Baytown Sun*, and she was a Baytonian success story. She made it out of Baytown and broke the small-town mold. She was the first woman to graduate from her university with a degree in electrical electronics engineering and went on to get her master's degree in business from Pepperdine University. She left a promising career at the Johnson Space Center to join the military. After twenty-three years, my mother retired as a decorated lieutenant colonel who met with heads of state, worked on classified missions, and traveled to some of the most dangerous and exotic places on earth.

I couldn't figure out why every promotion she got or what we did overseas was newsworthy, but word traveled fast. By the time we landed and made the hour-long drive from the Houston Intercontinental Airport to Grandma's house, three-quarters of Baytown knew we were there. People didn't swarm her, and most were proud of what she was doing, but jealous gossip spread like fire because my mom was doing newsworthy things and because she was in the newspaper. Not having a husband made her an easy target. We couldn't go to the drug store without people speculating about what we got and why, and those rumors grew with the telling. Texas-sized secrets, on the other hand, could stay hidden for almost a lifetime. My grandmother spilled one of those secrets during a visit when I was fourteen years old, and it put a ragged tear in the comfy-Texas jeans part of my life.

I was in Texas at least twice a year, summer and Christmas, no matter where my mother was stationed. Grandma's house was in a nice, quiet neighborhood just a short walk to Whataburger and the convenience store for ice cream. Summers were hot and uncomfortably humid on the Texas coast—even in the shade. My grandfather, "MB" Sandling, had worked at the refinery and provided a good life for his family in a good part of Baytown. They had a double-lot yard and were the first family in their middle-class neighborhood to get a TV.

I don't remember MB—he died when I was four—but sometimes I have a fragment of a dream where rough, ebony hands pick me up.

MB was a popular and social guy who liked to relax with his friends after a long refinery shift. He collapsed after a night of playing poker and all evidence pointed to foul play. His autopsy revealed that he was poisoned, but they never caught his killer.

He left my grandma and his three daughters behind with a small inheritance, and his daughters gave their share of it to my grandma so she could buy the family home.

My grandmother was no wallflower; she was strong-willed and kept our family together. My mother had an older sister, Joyce, and a younger sister, Rich. Aunt Joyce was moderately tempered with occasional bursts of meanness. She also had an insane sandwich fetish, and whatever she ate had to be between two slices of bread: fried chicken, steak, gumbo, mac and cheese; no matter what it was, it took sandwich form. My other aunt, Rich, was the complete opposite. She was always nice to me, but was volatile, explosive, and mean to everyone else. She refused to work and was always short of money. She was my grandmother's favorite, and everyone knew it. Over the years, my grandmother gave Rich tens of thousands of dollars, clothes, food, and everything else you can imagine.

My grandmother was tough as nails with everyone, except me and Aunt Rich. She couldn't say no to us; the difference was, I never asked for anything. While Mom was away, my Aunt Rich talked my grandmother into signing her house over to her and putting it up as collateral to get her then-boyfriend out of prison. Aunt Rich got so far in debt that my grandma nearly lost the house. Mom got it back, put it in her name, and from that point on she paid all my grandma's bills.

The battle to get the house back, and the fight to get my aunt to pay back any of what she owed, created bad blood and a rift that's never fully healed. We had a big family in Baytown, and everyone weighed in and took a side. Most of them believed my mom put the house in her name because she was a greedy control freak. The truth was, taking over my grandmother's house and bills was the only way to protect her from being thrown out on the street, and it put a tremendous strain on our finances. Mom didn't care, but the part of the family robbing my grandma never got over it. They were still backbiting us the summer I was fourteen when I was down for a visit with my cousins. We had found chocolate in the kitchen. My grandma was already asleep, and unclaimed candy on the counter is a big score when you're a kid.

Rahn was the oldest. He unwrapped the chocolate bar; it had seven remaining breakable sections, and there is no good way to divide seven pieces of late-night chocolate between three kids with child logic. So, an argument ensued.

Rahn was seventeen and Keisha was fifteen. They were older and bigger than me, so I didn't get a say.

"I get more," Rahn said, "because I'm the oldest."

"Well, you're the stupidest," Keisha said, "so I get more."

In the end they agreed to divvy it up by age and Rahn snapped the chocolate bar into pieces. Rahn got four and Keisha got two.

"Here you go, Nikki," Rahn said, handing me the last piece of chocolate like he was doing me a favor.

"I hate when you call me Nikki. My name is Raven."

"So . . . you're sayin' you don't want it?"

"No. I'm saying give it to me and call me Raven."

We went outside to see if there were any fireflies, and they were everywhere; but it was late, and I was asleep the moment I fell into bed.

I woke up doubled over at 4:00 a.m. feeling like I was about to explode.

I ran to the one bathroom we had. Keisha was already there. I banged on the door until she let me in, and we quickly traded seats on the toilet.

Rahn ran in, saw me on the toilet with Keisha squirming and yelling, "I'm dying. Hurry," at me to get off because she needed another turn. So Rahn jumped into Grandma's old claw-foot tub, pulled the shower curtain closed, and the rest is family history.

We didn't know that Grandma was constipated that week, or that after eating the pieces of ex-lax she thought she needed and them not working right away that she threw the rest on the counter, gave up, and went to bed.

The noise from our battle with the bathroom—and the stench— woke Grandma up. After eating most of the laxative chocolate bar, she had fought her battles before we woke up to take over the bathroom. She was still in bad shape and thought she was dying.

The next day we were playing in the yard, and Rahn was still complaining about having to clean the tub.

"Well, you are the oldest," Keisha said, smirking. "And the oldest gets the most chocolate."

"Ugh. If you ate four pieces, it would have been you in there."

"Uh-uh," Keisha said. "No way."

Rahn and Keisha were as close as I was going to get to a brother and sister. My grandma was still hurting, but we had survived the ex-laxing and lived to play another day.

In fine southern tradition, if you got punished, you had to cut your own switch down for your whooping. Rahn was mischievous, and I never saw him get through one single day without a whooping—not one. We used to joke that he was the reason the old hickory tree in the front yard was always bare of branches by summer's end.

Summers at Grandma's house are supposed to be easy. There's no school and there should be no pressure, but I was beginning to understand just how dysfunctional my family was.

It was another hundred-degree, hundred-percent humidity day, and we were playing barefoot in the side yard when a white Oldsmobile pulled into the driveway. A man wearing a buckskin shirt and a long, red-and-white-feathered headdress got out.

I stopped spraying Rahn and Keisha with the garden hose, and we stood there watching as he was let into the house. It wasn't something you saw every day. I didn't know who he was. Rahn and Keisha didn't know either. I naturally assumed it had something to do with my mother's job.

"He looks just like the Pemmican Indian on the beef jerky bag," Rahn said, then he grabbed the hose and the water fight was game-on again.

We were laying on the dry grass in the sparse shade, and I was mostly dry when my mother came out to get me. "Raven, come inside," she said sternly.

"We're coming!"

"No, just you."

She brought me into the living room. The man we'd seen get out of the car in full Lakota ceremonial dress was sitting in my grandmother's plastic-covered antique chair by the phone. He was tall. He had pronounced cheek bones, dark hair divided into two long braids that went down to his waist, and so many beads, feathers, and adornments that he looked like royalty.

He stood to meet me. No one said a word. After a long, awkward pause, I took the initiative.

"Hello, sir. My name is Raven. It's nice to meet you." My grandma sat on the sofa, looking uncharacteristically guilty.

My mother was in the chair across from her, seething and as mad as I'd ever seen her. "This is your grandfather," she said, matter-of-factly. She wouldn't say anything else, despite my obvious confusion about this complete stranger being my grandfather. She wouldn't make eye contact with anyone.

Tears streamed down his face. I couldn't process what she meant. I thought my grandfather was dead. He took my hands in his hands. He was a weeping stranger to me, and it was a little creepy.

"Hello, young one. I am Red Hawk of the Lakota. I have searched for you for years," he said, gently squeezing my hands. "I looked and I looked. Now, by the grace of the Great Spirit, I have found you at last."

I didn't know what to say. Then it struck me. "You look just like my mom."

She flinched, and her fists balled up like she was ready to throw a punch.

He let my hands go and looked around the room. Then he held my shoulders, looked deeper into my eyes than anyone had ever done, and said, "Now that I have met you, I know we will meet again. I will show you who you are and the warrior you were meant to be, *Aŋpétu wašté*." It meant "good day" in Lakota Sioux. It sounded portentous, but I wasn't afraid. His words resonated with me.

He smiled, took up my hands again, kissed each one, and then he left.

When the door closed behind him, my grandma said, "We won't ever have to see him again."

"Why wouldn't we see him again?" I asked, but Grandma refused to answer any of my questions. Then she dismissed me with, "Go play outside." She wasn't about to give me understanding or closure.

Mom explained afterward that the gentleman we met wouldn't marry my grandma after she became pregnant because the tribe didn't approve of her and Red Hawk, and that the man in the headdress was my mother's real father.

Then Grandma gave him the ultimatum: "Marry me, or you'll never see these kids again."

My grandmother made good on her threat. This was before the Internet, cell phones, and GPS; when people could disappear if they chose to. He didn't marry her, and even though Red Hawk had tried to be a part of our lives, Grandma wouldn't let him.

I say kids, plural, because my grandmother had let Red Hawk believe my Aunt Joyce was also his; years later when my grandma had another health scare, we learned my Aunt Joyce's father was someone else, but that's another story.

I was shocked, confused, and frustrated. I wasn't who I thought I was. My cousins weren't related to me the way I thought they were, and my grandma was not who I thought she was. I didn't want to know my grandmother was a harlot. People make mistakes, I get that. But at a time when a teenager is finding their way, my foundation was blown apart.

The fact that Aunt Joyce had a different father meant my grandma had lied to my mother, Red Hawk, and possibly MB as well as the rest of our family. Red Hawk was seventy-three years old when I met him. He was denied a lifetime with us. It was the cruelest stroke my grandma could have dealt, and I never forgot it.

Mom reacted poorly to the news. She was furious at MB and so desperate for her mother's love that she couldn't fault her for what my grandma had done.

I couldn't figure out why she was angry at MB. MB knew two of his daughters weren't his, but he loved them and raised them as if they were his own. He raised them like a father should.

I was angry with my grandmother for never telling her.

Grandma had an intestinal blockage and thought the truth about the identity of Mom's father would be her deathbed confession. However, after a short stay in the hospital, Grandma's blockage was cleared, and she lived long past that day to the ripe old age of ninety-six.

When townsfolk talked about my grandma, she claimed they were just jealous of her long, beautiful hair and her Native American features. I was ashamed to find out about her scandals. My grandmother was thirty-three years old when my mother was born, so these were not the actions of a scared teenager.

I saw my Native American grandfather once more at a reservation. He was an elder. We came out for a ceremony that was magical, and we were treated like royalty because the tribe recognized us as his heirs. He said our people originally came from South Dakota before the government relocated them. Mom was in uniform. I got the sense that she was a source of his pride, but she couldn't bear it, and we left soon after.

Mom had trouble forgiving her "father." She took my grandmother's maiden name, and became Major, then Lieutenant Colonel Friel, but I hated it. I didn't want a different last name than my mother, but life moved on.

My mom was fiercely private and had been secretly dating someone almost my entire life. After Germany, it was official, and I could call him Dad. It took less getting used to than I thought it would. I dismissed certain similarities and physical features we shared as coincidence. He's charismatic, good-looking, and an avid history buff. He was also an alpha male Air Force officer and mom's former boss. My middle name is Nichole, and sometimes I'd get called Nikki, which I despise. I don't know if he knew that, but from day one, he called me Nickel. He said it dramatically, like he was bestowing a call sign, and it stuck. Even today his calls start, "Hey, Nickel. You good?"

My parents' duties took them away from me, and they were gone more than they were home, but I made new friends. I studied nonstop and had skipped two grades, so when I turned sixteen, I left for college at Purdue University in West Lafayette, Indiana; and for the first time, I felt like I made it. I had a social life, people to talk to, and things to do. I had my own dorm room and mini-fridge. It was a welcome change from the isolation and loneliness of my childhood.

I went to my first college mixer, and we danced the "Electric Slide" and "Macarena," and laughed and ate until it hurt. I remember thinking it was the happiest I had ever been.

I had only been on campus three days when, a couple of hours into the mixer, campus security and the local police interrupted the party, tapped me on the shoulder, and escorted me out.

This is the day I had feared since my childhood. I thought, *Is Mom dead?* I asked questions; the authorities said nothing. I was scared and started to panic.

"Am I getting kicked out of school? What did I do?"

Nothing.

"What's happening here? What's this all about?"

"Ma'am. We have to go. Now."

I was hauled out of my dance like a criminal, given just enough time to throw a few things in a duffle bag, and had to put on a puddle jumper for a turbulent flight through thunderstorms.

My mother was waiting for me at the airport. She was in uniform.

I could feel her tension. "What's wrong?"

"Get in the car. We need to talk." My relief to see her alive was over-shadowed by fear.

But she didn't talk, and I had had enough. "Stop the car now. I was dancing and then—"

"I didn't want to do this, Raven, but we need to change your name. Now."

"Why? Why now?"

"You have to understand," she said, appraising me. "There are people who will hurt you to hurt us."

"What do you mean?" She was dead serious when she said it.

"Raven, serving this country, being in the military, is an honor . . . but sometimes that service comes at a high price. I can't tell you most of what your father and I do because it's classified, but there is true evil in this world. Evil most people will never know about or believe exists. I have seen things that would scare you to death."

"Why don't you change your name, then? I didn't do anything."

"I've tried to keep this away from you, but there are sick people out there, and right now, anonymity is the best protection we can give you."

"Can't we just change my social security number?"

"No. That wouldn't work."

"Mom. You're scaring me."

"I wish I could have seen you at the dance in your lavender dress; I rarely get to see you in girl clothes. It was your first dance. You were never interested in them before, but you had a such good time. I'm glad you have friends like Candace and Beth."

"How do you know that? I haven't told you their names yet."

"I got a call on a secure line at work from a man I didn't know with a thick Middle Eastern accent. He described the party in detail as well as what you were wearing and who you were with. Then he told me not to worry about you getting home. He said he would make sure you got home safely. In pieces. Starting with your lips."

My heart pounded and my blood ran cold. I had never felt so scared and unaware. Those words burned into me.

I didn't sleep that night. I'm in my forties now, and I can count the times I've slept peacefully through an entire night on one hand.

As we pulled into the courthouse parking lot, she continued, "That's when I arranged to get you out. Now we have to keep moving."

"It's your secret job. Why am I the only one changing my name? I didn't do anything wrong!" The phrase "It's not fair!" had the gravity of a black hole. I felt like I was paying for someone else's sin.

"I told you what he said, Raven. If you want to be safe, we need to go in now."

I cried in the car. I thought I'd stopped, but I could barely see the paperwork through my tears. Mom kept saying it would be okay, but I wasn't okay. There were already notarized papers in the stack and the court approved my name change that same day. Everyone was in on it but me. The judge made me confirm my new name. It was the first time I ever heard it.

Because of that—for my safety—my mother changed my name. I felt like I was excommunicated from my own family. That I was an outcast. A liability.

I became Dallas Nichole Sandling with the stroke of a pen.

I walked into the courthouse as me; I left as someone else.

"We chose Dallas because it was nebulous enough to be a boy or a girl," my mother said. "And you know, Sandling was my maiden name."

"The one you didn't want when you found out MB wasn't your father," I said sarcastically. Normally, sass like that—which, I admit, came naturally to me—would have earned a backhand to the face. She let it slide.

I drove home with my head on the passenger window glass, numb.

There was no debrief. No therapy.

"I don't want to go back to school, Mom, if I'm going to be watched or snatched away or raped over your job. How is that fair? How is any of this fair?"

"I never said it was fair. I said I was going to keep you safe."

"Great."

They never told me if they caught that psycho, only that it was finally safe for me to go back to Purdue. They took extra precautions at school. I just had to get through it, but I kept looking over my shoulder. How could I not?

Going back was awkward. Just days after introducing myself as Raven at Purdue and then getting dragged out of the dance and put in the back of a patrol car, I was now supposed to say, "Call me Dallas." The story was that my mom was in an accident, and they rushed me home. She was stable, so I came back, but I didn't want to talk about it.

Reintroductions, new IDs, different classes, more paperwork. For a while, the police not so subtly observed me, then campus security kept watch over me. I know it was for my protection, but it felt like I was a shoplifter they were following so they could catch me stealing pieces of my own life.

Then there was the way everyone treated my name change, like I'd gotten bored and changed it for attention, as though I was showing off a new piercing or tattoo. Even the professors. "Oh, that's right, you're Dallas now." Like it was my choice.

It faded but didn't stop. I was constantly reminding even dear friends, "I'm Dallas now," because I had no choice. It marred my school experience. It was the deciding factor for my leaving Purdue and starting fresh at another university.

We moved around. I came to terms with my name change. I understood I was still me. I was still Raven. The threats finally stopped, but I had been looking over my shoulder for so long that it was habit now.

I told Paul that story on our second date. It was his idea to change it back before we got married. It was like a great wrong had finally been righted and a monumental weight was lifted from my shoulders. I was happy, honored, and relieved to be Raven Harrison.

My childhood name change came up a few times on the campaign trail as a grasping-at-straws accusation. The first time it happened, I wasn't sure where they were going with it.

"So, I heard you changed your name," he said, with a *gotcha!* glint in his eye in the middle of the most influential contributors at the fundraiser.

"You heard? Okay, you got me," I said, smiling back. "I took my husband Paul's name when we got married."

I thought he was just another misogynist jerk making a snide comment.

"But you're hiding your identity."

"What are you talking about? I'm not hiding anything."

"Then who is Dallas Nichole Sandling?" he said, like he'd just found the smoking gun and solved a dinner theater mystery. He looked triumphant.

I don't know if he expected me to get defensive or cry or dry up and blow away. He certainly wasn't prepared for me laughing at him, and he shrank with all his bluster gone.

It took me a few seconds to get the words out. "Your big accusation is that my mom changed my name when I was a minor?" I had to laugh some more. "You do know kids aren't legally able to do that, right? I hope you're not a lawyer or running for office."

I knew people would run checks on me, and I welcomed it. My dad always says, "People with nothing to hide, hide nothing." I am no longer a defenseless child who has to hide. I have taken my life and my name back. I'm shocked at how many people with salacious and criminal backgrounds tried to use my public record name change to disparage me.

He slunk away, angry. I should really thank him. His big, Agatha Christie-reveal resulted in the biggest contributions my campaign had received at that point.

The COVID-19 lockdown disrupted everything. It was an unprecedented, unconstitutional government overreach that brought dark realities into the light. I had spent the last few years preoccupied with fixing the immediate problem, that my children weren't being taught the fundamentals they needed to learn in school.

Patience was a top student in her class, until she voted for Trump in a woke, school-sponsored, social justice experiment. I'll never forget the day I brought her home, when I was going through her curriculum, and I saw she was supposed to be learning geometry. At that point she was three-quarters of the way through the academic year.

I asked Patience, "What's a trapezoid? What's a rhombus?"

She didn't know.

"Patience. Do you know what geometry is?" Silence.

It was clear when I put Patience and Major in homeschool there were gaps in what they were supposed to have learned. Another example occurred when the kids were working through online math problems, and I had to take a call.

Major is two grades behind Patience, and she had just finished her assignments.

I muted the phone. Major was struggling. "Patience, please help Major with his long division and remainders."

"Okay," she said, then looked at me confused. "What's a remainder?"

She was in fourth grade. They were progressing through their homeschool syllabus, but I realized basic skills were still missing, and we had to get back to brass tacks.

In the middle of the endless COVID-19 lockdowns, I found Patience in her room staring at the computer. Her class had just ended, and I said, "What is it, honey?"

"I'm lonely." The light had gone out of her usually bright eyes, and my stomach sank. "I finished my work," she said, "but I miss my friends, and I miss school."

I thought I was doing a good job, but I was so focused on getting her education caught up that I had missed the element of socialization that comes from being around peers at school.

It was important. Kids need it. If I missed that, what else had I missed?

Seeing my daughter unhappy brought me to where I should have started. It was a Friday night, and I dropped to my knees and prayed, "God. I don't know what to do. I'm fighting as hard as I can. I'm fighting for my kids, but I'm failing. I'm trying to find them the best schools. I'm trying to give them the best education. I'm engaged, but I'm failing, and my kids are miserable."

I was lost.

"God, my son's not getting what he needs, and I seem to always be one step behind. I'm running from evil in the schools. I'm fighting as hard as I can.

"I support and respect his teachers, but he came home with a black eye. He's having trouble making friends. His teacher is encouraging kids to bully him because she says his mom has 'blackface.' My precious boy is suffering because I'm his mother.

"But I keep running right into one problem after the other, and I'm lost. If you've given me signs, I've missed them, and I don't know how to move forward to protect my family."

It was a hard and humbling conversation for me to have with God.

I grew up Catholic, with a solid sense of right and wrong, but I didn't have a relationship with God. I believed in Him with my whole heart. I feared Him, but I wasn't taught to listen for Him and to let Him guide me. When I was Catholic, I felt like I was just showing up on Sundays to learn how horrible a person I was. It didn't feel uplifting or inspiring.

I remember being reprimanded in Catholic school for asking why priests cannot marry if marriage is a holy institution. Ultimately, I switched to nondenominational church in college, and it has become the bedrock of my relationship with God.

I felt like God had made me strong and intelligent so I would know what to do.

I should know what to do. Take another step and keep moving forward, but as a mom it ate away at me.

I was willing to do anything.

I was about as humble and as low as you can get.

I was in tears. "Lord, what should I do?"

The very next day—on a Saturday evening, no less—the phone rang, and a prominent GOP official asked me to run for Congress.

He told me I could make a difference for my kids, for all kids.

Paul said it was what I was put on the Earth to do.

God heard the cry of His child and answered.

I remember looking up at the TV. Biden was stumbling through another COVID-19 message to the American people. More lockdowns. Mandatory vaccinations if you wanted to keep your job. He drifted off mid-thought. He didn't finish his sentences. He was pitting neighbor against neighbor. Caravans of illegal immigrants were pouring though our southern border in need of food, shelter, healthcare, and employment. But the economy was crumbling. Unprecedented supply chain issues were causing long delays and empty shelves at the grocery store.

I told Paul we were heading to communism.

He didn't believe me. Not at first.

I was seeing a mockery of everything my parents had fought for. After just a few months of having no real leadership at the helm, our country was faltering.

I woke early Sunday morning with one thought on my mind.

I would do what God had called me to do. I was running for Congress.

We bought a house in Frisco, Texas, in the northern suburbs of Dallas-Fort Worth. In 2017, Frisco was the fastest growing city in America, and even during COVID-19 it remained vibrant and open. After the shackles of California and Nevada restrictions, I was back in the land of the free and home of the brave, and it was liberating. My kids were in school, learning and socializing with friends, and in May of 2021, we touched down in Texas, and I took my first steps onto the campaign trail.

CHAPTER 7

CAMPAIGN TRAIL

"What counts is not necessarily the size of the dog in the fight—
it's the size of the fight in the dog."

Schoolhouse Rock! taught me how a bill becomes a law, but getting started in national politics— beyond a persuasive vision and drive—is about lawyers, money, and who you know. I knew I needed help to guide me through the process, but I didn't exactly know how to get there. I felt like Frodo Baggins in *The Fellowship of the Ring*, declaring, "I will take it! I will take the ring to Mordor. Though . . . I do not know the way."[1]

Substitute DC for Mordor, and well . . . you get the picture.

I needed an experienced campaign manager with strong party ties, a head for strategy and analytics, great organizational skills, a reliable fundraising history, and solid media connections. Like any good leader, they should know their own strengths and hire staff to complement their abilities and execute campaign operations.

Campaign managers are hired based on their skill set, familiarity with the battleground, level of commitment, and their ability to quickly adapt and build campaigns around their candidates. The very best campaign managers tend to be met through introductions or mutual interests. I was looking for an insider experienced with getting a candidate on the ballot, who was already familiar with Texas politics, and connected to conservative organizations in my district.

I was looking for a Republican campaign manager, not a unicorn; but even with referrals, finding one was tough. Regardless of where their offices were listed, every phone number led back to DC. I approached more than twenty individuals and offices. Even though they said they represented Republicans, they all had deep blue connections and funding. We'd talk. I'd ask who they got elected, and they were all Democrats.

They would say, "Don't worry, we handle both. We're objective. We are bipartisan. We're everything you want and need." I listened to a lot of pitches that, if I'm being honest, were like time-share pitches without the free lunch.

That's another aspect of politics: something's always in play, and someone's always being played. That's why a personal network of people you can trust to deliver is everything.

But I'm a good researcher, and I sifted through all the consultant spin and lawyer speak. There were a few questions that should have been easy to answer like, "Hey, have you actually gotten a Republican elected?", or "Do you have offices in any red state?", or "What services do you provide for how much? And what can I expect, today, tomorrow, in a month?"

Most answers were a tediously long version of, "It depends," and I whittled a few dozen prospects down to three that looked solid with strong party endorsements: one in Florida, one in South Dakota, and one in Dallas with ties to Rudy Giuliani.

Florida and Dallas got back to me.

Florida spent the call asking me what the political landscape and climate were for my congressional race, what my strategy was, how I intended to run the campaign, and my plan to hire staff. They offered no options or solutions. That's why I needed a campaign manager, to provide the experience I lacked and manage my campaign.

They seemed genuinely surprised when I said it didn't seem like a good fit.

The Dallas consultant's name was Mitch Sergeant. I gave him the elevator speech. My parents are retired US Air Force lieutenant colonels. I'm a native Texan, mom, wife, patriot, and business owner. I told him I was going to fight the betrayal of America, and I told him why and how and what I had done to establish myself.

Mitch told me about his clients, dropped a bunch of high-profile names that seemed to check out, and outlined what he would do to get me started, assemble the team, and run my campaign.

He sounded like exactly what we needed. He was in Dallas, not far from where our house would be, and I paid him a big retainer to get started. We scheduled our first meeting and then I took Patience and Major to Cracker Barrel to celebrate with a Texas-style breakfast.

I had everything invested in Mitch because I didn't know where to start. We met, and he already had a plan outlined. Mitch was great at outlines. "Got it. Don't worry. I know Trump. I know the guy who did this and that."

He did know them, so I thought we were in good shape. He came across as bona fide and bankable, but then Mitch said, "We need you to join some clubs and get involved."

I said, "Put me in coach. I'm ready to play. I'm thinking Texas GOP auxiliary organizations like the Texas Cavalry!" And he tells me to start signing up at grocery stores.

"Get rewards cards from H-E-B and Kroger? Is that really what you mean by clubs?"

"You need to establish yourself across the community."

"You got to be freaking kidding me." I was trying to wrap my head around what he was saying. I was skeptical and trying to weigh what I was hearing against the fact that we paid him a lot of money for his expertise, and what's the point of hiring people if you don't listen to the advice they give? I thought he was eccentric.

What I didn't know then was that I was already on the radar of those seeking to maintain the status quo, and that Mitch was getting paid to waste my time and run down my campaign clock to election day.

At the beginning, I didn't see his game. He had me go to a Faith in Freedom conference and that was a great experience. It introduced me to high-profile people across the GOP and in Christian organizations. It also gave me a chance to socialize my position on different issues with conservative leaders across the United States. I was finding my voice and making connections when Mitch said, "Shake hands, take pictures, get in front of everyone. Just make sure you don't tell people you're running for Congress."

"Isn't that the point? Why not?"

"Because you don't want a target on your back," said Mitch. "You don't want everyone gunning for you until you've got everything set up and everyone in place."

It made sense, barely, but it cut against my grain. I felt like I had my foot on the accelerator while I was pulling the emergency brake.

"First, we need to get you a campaign manager."

That blindsided me. "I thought you were my campaign manager?"

"No," he said. "I'm your general counsel, helping you get your campaign organized."

"Okay? That's important to know."

"And we need to get you a fundraiser."

"How does fundraising work?" I'd raised capital for business ventures, but political rules were different.

"You just have to set aside some seed money to get started," said Mitch. "And then you hire a manager and pay yourself back through your fundraising."

"Got it. Our priorities are finding and hiring a campaign manager and a fundraiser to get ahead of the redistricting decision." Redistricting redraws the political maps that lay out voting districts. It occurs following an updated census. Texas's redistricting occurred in July of 2021, but I couldn't officially file until November. Mitch's plan was based on the presumption that Republicans were going to fight to secure new congressional seats based on the population explosion revealed in the census.

"Do you have leads for those positions?"

"I already have calls in," said Mitch. "I have a campaign manager in mind who was an organizer for Trump's campaign in Texas. I think he'll be a good fit."

"Good. And fundraisers?"

"I already have a lead on one. I know this state senator who's not looking for reelection. I'm friends with his fundraiser, and she's a strong producer."

"Okay. Both sound good. When can I meet them?"

"Give me a week."

A week turned into next week. Next week turned into a month. We were having daily calls while moving from Nevada to Texas. "Mitch, what are we doing this week? What can I be doing before the kids go to school?"

"I got a call to this guy—"

"Where's the fundraiser? When do we meet these people?" It wasn't just me losing my cool. My husband was getting anxious about the checks we were writing, and this was on top of relocating our jobs and moving across the country with two kids.

I was done with his excuses, and sensing my frustration, Mitch started having me attend fundraisers for prominent Republicans.

I didn't waste time stroking egos and telling them how great they were. I asked questions, shared credentials, and really got a sense of who they were and who the real fighters were. Two of the greats are Texas Agriculture Commissioner Sid Miller and Attorney General Ken Paxton. Sid Miller is a staunch patriot, solid conservative, and a gentleman. If he gives you his word, you can take that to the bank. He loves this country, and I am honored to call him a friend.

AG Paxton is also a frontline fighter. As he is General Paxton, he began calling me the Colonel. AG Paxton is in the trenches every day fighting the swamp on a level most people cannot imagine. I am honored to be an ally to these and other freedom fighters.

I met other good Texans who bear witness to the betrayal of America's values: the patriots and veterans fighting to turn the tide of liberalism with liberty, inequity with justice, and to fight the insipid fear pervading our society with constitutional protections.

I met no-kidding GOP movers and shakers, had honest conversations, and we shared many of the same concerns.

I was finally getting my name, face, and ideas out there and getting involved. People were learning the kind of person I am, but without a campaign manager and fundraiser, my campaign felt bogged down to the axels in mud and spinning its wheels. It wasted months of the most valuable resource I had: time.

I was meeting people in all the grassroots clubs. Everyone was buzzing about how Biden's administration was everything we worried it would be, but there was also excitement building at the local level that we could drive real change starting as soon as the next primaries.

But Mitch's counsel to me was, "Don't tell people you're running. Get them to encourage you to run, but don't say a thing." I thought it was an odd approach when I needed to start building coalitions.

"Where are we on my campaign manager?" I asked.

"We're talking, and I'm close to bringing him in."

My sighs were becoming groans and growls.

"I think it's time you meet a superb fundraiser. Come with me. I'm heading there now."

I did, and I liked her. She was delightful, beautiful, pleasant, and came highly recommended.

Then another week passed with no fundraiser. "Mitch, what's happening with her?"

"She doesn't think you have enough experience."

"Seriously? That's interesting." I had researched her and discovered that she was the first cousin of a sitting Congressman. "So she got her job through nepotism, and she's seriously questioning whether I can do a job?"

Silence. Mitch was floored.

"What's really going on?"

It was a question Mitch didn't like.

"Mitch?"

"No fundraiser wants to work with you because they don't want to go against an incumbent."

"Why do they think we're running against an incumbent?"

It wasn't a question Mitch could or would answer.

I didn't recognize it then, but it was my first indication of corruption and that my party was pushing back on me.

The district was in the process of being rezoned. Nothing had been officially released yet, Mitch's invoices were still coming in, and now, no fundraisers wanted to work with me.

By Mitch's reckoning, the best and brightest GOP warriors were fighting for the new districts to be redrawn Republican red. Based on the recent census, they were forecasting two, possibly three, new seats for Texas's Congressional Districts.

Political operatives on the left have a very real strategy to help relocate like-minded coastal liberals to Texas, with the goal of flipping Texas blue. Coupled with a lack of federal enforcement and Democrat border policies designed to destabilize Texas and Florida, the changing congressional demographics will disproportionately impact Texas.

In March, when I started communicating with Mitch, Plan A was for me to run for office in one of the new districts. It appeared likely we would get a seat in an area with a strong Republican base because our conservative district had the highest population growth in Texas.

Plan B was for me to campaign in District Twenty-Six against the eighteen-year incumbent, Dr. Michael Burgess, if he ran for reelection, but there were whispers that he might not. At the time it seemed like we were a shoo-in for Plan A—my congressional run for a newly minted seat.

Every time I asked, "Mitch, where do you think they'll draw the lines?" he sent me a different proposed map, but the new lines didn't sync with the census data, and we went to the redistricting meeting.

"My buddy, Michael, heads this up," Mitch said as we found our seats. "This is gonna be great. Dallas-area Republicans are going to fight hard for it."

I thought, *Fantastic. Go Team Red!*

Only my Republican brethren proposed a ridiculous map I had never seen before. One that drew the new district to Austin, which is as blue as the swamp is deep, and another one down to Houston, which currently identifies as Democrat, and it's getting bluer.

"Hang on," I said. "You guys said you were fighting for a new district."

A member of the redistricting committee addressed me. "Young lady," she said in a condescending tone. "It's rather complicated."

"Really? You rolled over and caved to the left. Complicated how? There was more population growth here in the Dallas-Fort Worth area, per the census. Why don't we have the district?"

I wasn't the only person in the room surprised, but I had Mitch going, "Raven. Take it easy."

"They took it easy. You said our Republicans were fighting for that new district, but not only did they not fight, I didn't even hear an argument, and they didn't answer my question. Now whatever backdoor deal they made behind the scenes is going forward."

I couldn't shake the feeling that the fundraisers had already known how the new districts would be drawn.

In the end, I let God decide what district I'd campaign in when I picked our house. We had to finish our move and get the kids in school. Even with all the bluster, secret deals, and gerrymandering, we barely made it into the district: Texas's Twenty-Sixth Congressional District.

"Okay, Mitch, what's the play?"

"We have a solid Plan B."

"Alright, we're going into twenty-six instead of a new district. What's our strategy?"

"We gotta hurry up and get you a campaign manager. I already have someone interested."

"Agreed," I said (and you already know how that was going). "When do I meet your new guy?"

Mitch was watching people leave the room, stealing glances at us, curious as to who I was. "I want to meet with Burgess first." .

"What for?"

"To see if he's even running. Rumors are he's undecided. Let's just see if, maybe, he would pass the baton to you as a solid conservative. If he's not gonna run again, there's no sense reinventing the wheel." The problem was that Dr. Burgess was not a solid conservative. He had a bluish-purple voting record, had been flagged for insider trading, and had said on national television that fetuses in utero can " . . . put their hands between their legs. If they can feel pleasure, they can feel pain," which made me physically sick to hear. He is also the only "Republican" who voted with Nancy Pelosi and the Democrats to lower the voting age to sixteen.

"I don't really think this is a good idea. It seems like he puts that retirement rumor out every election to see who will run against him."

"It's our best move, Raven. Let's just start there."

"Fine. I question the timing, but whatever you say."

Mitch set up the meeting, but immediately started to backpedal. "It's scheduled early in the morning. I'm gonna see if I can get a better time slot."

"No, Mitch. The time's fine."

"It is like 8:00 a.m. Traffic's gonna be horrible."

"It doesn't matter. We'll just leave early and grab a coffee or something until he gets there."

Unbeknownst to me, Mitch went and bitched about the time to Burgess's secretary. So our appointment was dismissed.

I found out the night before.

"We're not having the meeting tomorrow. Sorry it didn't work out. I was trying to get you a better time, for your kids."

I was furious. "You weren't getting it for me, Mitch. You changed it because you didn't want to get your lazy ass up." I fought down the urge to fire him on the spot, but I'd already paid for deliverables he still owed me. "Don't ever do that again. I won't say it again."

He nodded and rescheduled the meeting a couple of weeks later.

The crucial difference was when we first had the meeting scheduled, the filing deadline hadn't opened for congressional candidates. We had our rescheduled meeting with District Twenty-Six incumbent, Dr. Burgess, after it opened. He still hadn't announced whether he would run again, and Mitch claimed he was still hearing rumors that he would not.

We were moving into our new home and getting organized for the campaign. November 13, 2021, was the first day you could file as a candidate to get on the ballot for the March 1, 2022, US House Texas District Twenty-Sixth Republican primary.

"What do I need to do to file?"

"Let me look into it," said Mitch.

"What do you mean? You said you've done this before." His resume was full of people he had gotten elected in Texas and the incumbents he'd ousted. They were highlighted parts of his resume he'd marked with gold stars, and this was the easy part. It was the first time I questioned his actual influence on those elections, but it wouldn't be the last.

In essence, to become a candidate is to overcome the bureaucracy a state has imposed to keep you out. You find and download the form(s) from the secretary of state's website, fill them out, have them notarized, and either get thousands of signatures—which I wasn't willing to risk— or pay $3,000. In my case, that money went to the Republican Party of Texas to file for Congress. It was a deliberate, tiresome barrier to entry with a surprising amount of drama.

After waiting for Mitch to walk us through the filing process, we went for our own walk, got the paperwork together, filled it out, and had it notarized. My husband and three volunteers cross-checked it against the requirements before we submitted it, and I lined out that task on my "Raven for Congress" to-do list.

Two days later, we got a call from the filing office. On the line was a polite woman who was very sorry to tell me that the candidacy form they received was missing required notary information, and they couldn't accept it.

During our discussion, it turned out my form was in fact notarized with the right signature in the proper place, and I thought the issue was resolved.

The next day, the polite woman called again. "We reviewed your updated application, thank you. But you filled out the wrong form, and we can't accept it."

"What do you mean?" I was confused. "I filled out the secretary of state form you specified."

My husband overheard the conversation. He's pilot-level meticulous and a stickler for details. He had downloaded the forms and sat beside me with his copies.

"I'm afraid you filled out the wrong form," said the nice lady, now on speakerphone. "It's supposed to come from the secretary of state's website."

"Good. That's exactly where it came from."

"Let me put you on hold for a moment."

"Oh," she said, returning. "You need a form dated after 2019."

"We're good then," I said. "I'm looking at a copy of the form we submitted, dated September of 2021." Paul shuffled through the forms, shaking his head in disbelief. Every section was filled out properly.

"Ah," she said returning. "You need the form that says, 'You have not been convicted of a felony.'"

"Yes, I do. It's checked and signed off. I'm looking at an exact copy. Did you even look at my application?"

"Let me put you on hold." She was noticeably less polite.

"You're kidding, right?" They weren't going to accept my legally signed, notarized, and completely executed package.

"Oh, actually, you've got form A. It needs to be form B."

"Really? Standby a sec." Paul printed off the form. "Funny thing. I'm looking at form B. It's almost identical, but it's missing the boxes you said I must sign-off to confirm I've never been convicted and that I'm legally eligible to run for office. Tell me, how do you propose I do that if it's not on the form?"

There was a long pause.

"What's really going on here? Because it seems like you're trying to stop me from becoming a candidate."

That's when our line disconnected.

The registration process to get on the ballot was a clown show. I was fuming. Paul went through all the forms with a microscope. We had addressed everything.

I followed up with the filing office. I couldn't get through.

They sent back my check and rejected my application for it not being on the right form with the right boxes checked and signed, even though it was.

I sent both Form A and B back—signed, notarized, sealed—with a new check and by registered mail. I also let them know that we would give the press a statement if it was rejected again for complying with their rules. Finally, it went through.

It was my first taste of political weirdness. It wouldn't be the last.

I couldn't even file without controversy, but file I did. I was officially a Republican Party candidate for the Texas District Twenty-Six race for Congress. I was on the ballot.

CHAPTER 8

=====

COFFEE WITH THE ENEMY

"Early is on time, on time is late, and late is unacceptable."
—Lieutenant Colonel John Paul (Zeb) Zebelean III,
USAF (ret), a.k.a Dad

Four days later, we met Dr. Burgess at an upscale coffeehouse in Dallas. Mitch and I were going over talking points and our objectives when he said, "He's coming with his fundraiser."

I had a bad feeling. "Mitch, I think you're the only one who still believes he isn't running."

"Do you still want to go through with this meeting?"

"We should see what his plan is, obviously, but if he's coming with his fundraiser, he intends to run again."

Dr. Burgess arrived with his fundraiser, a woman whose name I don't recall; after an exchange of handshakes and coffee orders, we settled into a corner table.

I sat diagonal from Dr. Burgess, with Mitch sitting directly in front of him chatting and dropping names of prominent Republicans they knew.

Burgess nodded his head to the beat of Mitch's banter, but he was nervously side-eying me. By the time Burgess started tapping his foot in annoyance, Mitch was done strolling down memory lane, and Burgess's eye was twitching. I felt like I was making him uncomfortable, but I hadn't said a word so I couldn't figure out why.

Finally, Mitch got to the point. "Well, Dr. Burgess, it has been great catching up." From the expression on Burgess's face, it didn't seem great for him. "Your time is valuable. What we really want to ask is, are you planning on running again?"

At that, Dr. Burgess changed from timid and mildly annoyed to incensed. "I'm vaccinated, signed, sealed, and delivered! You bet I'm running again!"

Okay, I'm thinking. *That was an oddly strong response. Interesting. That answers that.* I have an impenetrable poker face and outwardly showed nothing.

Then Burgess looked me dead in the eye. "Wait a minute. Are you thinking of running?" As I hadn't said a single word, I was surprised by his insolent tone.

"I'm thinking about a lot of things," I said, mustering a level of respect he wasn't showing me. I found him patronizing. It was fore-shadowing.

"Let me tell you something, missy," he said, leaning on the table and glaring. "This district is affluent, sophisticated, and educated. I'm their guy. They'll never accept you."

Really? I remembered thinking. *So this is the esteemed Congressman Burgess?* He's been in office since 2003 and hasn't accomplished a single thing, and I came here out of respect. "Missy?" I said, enraged. "Who the *hell* do you think you're talking to?"

His fundraising manager actually gasped.

Burgess shrank as his Minnesota-born sensibilities got a Texas 101 lesson: mess with the bull, you get the horns.

Mitch turned red, then purple, like he was having a stroke. "Uh, Raven—"

I cut him off and stood. "Don't 'Raven' me. It's him. You know he's insulting me, right?" And I locked on Burgess. "Missy? Listen up, *grandpa.* I live in this affluent, sophisticated, and educated district." The gloves were off. "How dare you speak to me about affluence and sophis-tication? My parents and husband were military officers. They have bled for this country and given it more than your sorry ass ever will. I was born in Texas, right here on the soil you claim to represent. You don't know me, and you have the gall to look down your nose at me?"

His nervous twitch was gone. What remained on his face was snarling arrogance. "I can't be beaten. I've delivered half the babies in this county."

"Now you want to stick a needle in their arm with an unproven vac-cine. How does that work?" If he'd been the "doctor" that delivered my children, I'd be asking for a refund. "So if someone needs a C-section on the House floor, you're their guy. Otherwise, what have you done for Twenty-Six other than enrich yourself?"

But he didn't have an answer—not one he wanted to share with the other coffee drinkers watching the show.

"I don't know what kind of women you're used to,"—looking at his fundraiser,—"but you don't get to talk like that to me. Whatever respect I had for you is gone."

I stood and said, "Have a nice day," and left the meeting with Burgess's and the packed coffee shop-goers' jaws on the floor and Mitch chasing after me.

"Are you alright?" Mitch asked, catching up. "Oh my God, Raven." Mitch had never seen me go off.

"Yeah." That idiot is my congressman. "I've dealt with arrogant people like him in business for years. At least we confirmed he's running."

With that auspicious start, my campaign really began.

Burgess was a disappointing narcissist and an entrenched politician. I felt good about standing my ground. That must have been how Trump felt, standing up to the establishment.

Mitch and I went next door to the Capital Grill to debrief our meeting. It was one of Mitch's favorite places: crisp tablecloths, heavy silverware, honest pours.

After meeting Burgess, I felt surprisingly good about taking our next step. Mitch, on the other hand, seemed rattled.

"I told you this was gonna be difficult," said Mitch, motioning to a waiter. Actually, he hadn't. "But at least we got to talk."

"You didn't tell me it was going to be difficult. You said we were getting a new district, remember? Were you in the same meeting I was? That guy's a joke. He actually said he was there for the committee assignments. He is there for himself, not his constituents. Twenty-Six deserves better. We have to do this."

"Yes," Mitch said. "We do."

"Okay, then. Is that twitch because he's old, or because he took the vaccine?"

"You know, Twenty-Six is going to love your fire."

"I'm ready to bring it. I didn't underestimate him; he underestimated me."

I was expecting: "Nice job, Raven. I'm proud you stood your ground."

Instead, I got: "I thought you'd get that rezoned district. Now, we're up against King Kong."

———

Mitch called the next day. "Burgess is mad at me."

"Who the hell cares that Burgess is mad. What is this? Middle school?" It didn't sit right. "Hey, when did you talk to Burgess?"

Mitch hemmed and hawed. He was an outline-driven kind of legal consultant. It was uncomfortable hearing him all over the place mouthing talking points that weren't his. It wasn't a long conversation, and it bothered me that he seemed more concerned with Burgess's feelings than my campaign, but I set that aside. The meeting with Burgess was his idea.

Burgess was the incumbent, and my run for Congress was now an uphill battle, but my military parents had taught me that to win battles, you have to understand and control the shape of the battlefield.

I filed away the fact that Burgess was pissed off. Four candidates filed to run against him; was he mad at all of them? Or only me? I looked forward to using that in our debate in a similar way to how Trump took advantage of Hillary Clinton's arrogance and condescension to throw her off her game.

Two weeks later, Mitch called again. "You know, I think you should run for county commissioner."

"You're kidding, right? I've already filed. I'm on the ballot. I've got a website."

"It would be a slam dunk and a solid next step," he said. "You could prepare for your congressional run and make connections while you run out a commissioner term. It would position you for the seat after Burgess moves on."

"I'm out there. I'm going to events. Who thinks I should run for county commissioner?"

"Well, we've been talking."

"Who's we?"

"It doesn't matter."

"Yes, it does. It matters to me. Who are you discussing my campaign with, Mitch?"

There was a long pause.

"Who? Tell me who thinks I should be the dogcatcher instead of running for Congress."

"A sitting congressman you haven't met."

"Why does this congressman give a damn what I do? I'm not running against him. Shouldn't he focus on his own race?"

"He and Burgess are friends."

"And you and he are friends. So what? Tell me Mitch, why is this mystery congressman advising you about my campaign without my knowledge or consent? It sounds like what you're saying is, 'If he can get me to stop running against Burgess, then maybe Burgess owes him a favor in Congress.'"

"Welcome to politics. Sure you don't want to be county commissioner?"

"I'm not even going to dignify that with an answer."

"We'll be taking the long road to Congress then."

"Through swamp as far as the eye can see. You still on board?"

I heard a long sigh, then Mitch answered, "Yes."

Texas's Twenty-Sixth US Congressional District is north of Dallas-Fort Worth and includes most of Denton County as well as Cooke and Wise County. Denton is one of the wealthiest counties in Texas, and Cooke and Wise are rural—mostly agricultural and ranches. Both counties are growing and, as of my bid for Congress, the district's population was over 940,000 with a few more females than males, over 61 percent white, almost 20 percent Hispanic, and the black and Asian populations under 10 percent each.

I spoke across Denton County, and I genuinely enjoy participating in grassroots events, listening to what our different communities need, and the spirited debate between candidates and constituents. I had the opportunity to discuss my experiences and how I would address issues important to us all if I were elected to Congress.

I have business, executive, and foreign policy experience. I've balanced a budget in the tens of millions. I've spent time in DC. I have patriots on my side. I have strong military and veteran support. Every candidate wanted to fix our country, but I had actual experience and a plan I could articulate to get there.

I was also the only Texas-born candidate trying to represent Texan values.

During one speaking event, a candidate became so tongue-tied, he ran out of time, and no one could understand his message. The candidate before him read from the Bible nonstop the entire time, and I was feeling pretty good about where I stood in the race. My message was getting through, and my events were exciting.

I remember being in the meet-and-greet phase of one event, talking to people who really cared about America and were worried about where it was heading when an energy guy, who was also a candidate for Congress's Twenty-Sixth District, pulled me aside and said, "You should know, the Denton County Republican Party chair is telling everyone you're a Democrat plant."

I was gobsmacked. I had never even spoken to the party chair.

Before that moment, I was attending district-wide events. After the establishment labeled me a Democrat plant, I was suddenly left off all the event invitations and listings in voters' guides that all the other candidates received, and several of the party's elected precinct chairs suddenly didn't want to let me in on anything or see me at their functions and fundraising events.

I reached out to our local party leadership to get resolution, but I was ignored.

I wasn't on the guest list anymore, but I was still a congressional candidate on the ballot, and there was only one thing left to do.

Crash the events.

My team got good at event triage. And it had to be triage because by the time I found out about an event, there was little to no time to prepare and get there. I was like a storm chaser, only for meet and greets, debates, and forums.

Sometimes I'd screech to a stop in a parking lot with just enough time to adjust my clothes and walk in as they were closing the doors to start, but I was there.

The other candidates had five people working each event. Everyone else on the ballot had literature, yard signs, and swag. Usually, I had nothing, and if I did come with people and things to give away, the table we'd get was far from any action.

I literally had to show up and tell people I was running, even though I was the second person to file. The other candidates filed after me, yet my own party wouldn't tell me what was happening.

I heard, "I didn't know you were running," from the event organizers I confronted.

I'd answer, "How could you not? It was published in the paper. Every candidate is listed. And, yes, you do know." I expected it from the progressives, the left, and the Democrat party. But these were my own people—supposed anti-corruption stumping conservative Republicans from the great state of Texas. They would have slammed the door in my face if they thought they could get away with it. But I did show up, and their bouncer's velvet rope was grudgingly dropped to let me in.

We were spending a ton of money, and Mitch still couldn't find a campaign fundraiser. I had lost confidence in Mitch. I was slowly disentangling him from my operation. I had hired Lauren, a friend I met through my church as my campaign manager, which was stellar . . . only she actually added to my workload, filling my to-do list with tasks I didn't know I needed to do. She had no political experience, but neither did I, and she was a marketing maven, willing to roll up her sleeves and fight with me. All the other candidates were getting help from grassroots movements or the auxiliary and coalition organizations that work with the Republican Party.

Meeting with those organizations to share my vision and spread the word had become a priority. I was being frozen out of events, but my campaign was making progress in other areas, so I called, wrote, and visited every local political organization that I could, but it was mostly crickets.

CHAPTER 9

MENTOR

"Perseverance is the hard work you do after you get
tired of doing the hard work you already did."
—Newt Gingrich[1]

I crashed a Friday event, and one of the Wise County conservative organizers pulled me aside. "I didn't even know you were running, you're so good. I don't know how you got left off the invitation, but we have a gala tomorrow, and you simply must come."

A gala requires more preparation than tomorrow. I said, "I have plans, tomorrow is my husband's birthday." I didn't even look at the invitation she handed me.

"It's going to be big," she said with a dazzling smile.

And even my campaign manager, Lauren said, "We should go."

"No, I—"

They talked me into it. I tried everything to get out of it, but I'm glad Lauren made me go. It was meant to be, and it changed my life. Bishop Archer was the keynote speaker. I didn't know he was speaking. I didn't know anything about him.

Everyone was in fancy black-tie apparel, the event was packed, and, of course, all my competitors had booths and people taking their yard signs and campaign literature. My competitors had their spouses to campaign for them; my spouse was home alone with our kids celebrating his birthday without me. I was fighting twice as hard to appear credible despite a coordinated effort to marginalize me.

It was starting to get to me. Being the only candidate kept out of the loop. In the dark on every event. Scrambling to make it to everything. The weight of it all had grown heavy and difficult to bear.

I was in a bad mood. I had tried to celebrate Paul's birthday before the gala, but it felt like I was just going through the motions, and I loved his birthday. I'd put on Race2theRaven events in cities across America to celebrate it, but for the first time, I felt no joy. We arrived an hour late, missed the dinner, and they still charged me full price. I think even Lauren was beginning to regret pushing so hard to get me there.

We had finally made it in, but of course, it was a capacity crowd. Bishop Archer had already reached the podium and began to speak.

A group of veterans was sitting in the back at a table, and Lauren whispered to the elderly man next to two open seats, "Can we sit here with you?"

And in that packed room, with Bishop Archer about to passionately testify on stage, the elderly gentleman shouted, "What did you say?!" because he was hard of hearing.

Lauren turned beet red and had already sunk into her seat when every head in the room turned to look at me.

It felt like even Bishop Archer stopped talking, and my heart skipped a beat.

I thought, *This day just gets better and better.* It was 8:00 p.m. I would rather be anywhere else. I couldn't wait for the event to be over.

Then I listened to the bishop's testimony, and I was moved. It was like he was talking directly to me. He talked about overcoming the three abortion attempts on his life: his mother was beaten, given an overdose of pills, and finally assaulted with a white-hot poker and unimaginable hardship. His words spoke to my soul, reminding me of who I was as a pro-life advocate and what I was fighting for.

Afterward, he came down from the stage and everyone—and I mean everyone—lined up to shake his hand. That's what you do in politics. You meet everyone. You shake every hand, and you try to get all the help you can.

He walked past them all, came straight to me, and stopped.

It created a stir.

I was stunned. I stood, extended my hand like I was supposed to, ready to say, "Hi, I'm Raven, and I'm running for . . ." But my mind went blank. It wasn't that I was nervous. My mouth opened, but no words came out and everything stood still. God wanted me to listen, and I did.

Bishop Archer took my hand in his and said, "I'm your confirmation," and it was as though a spell was broken and people began to chatter again. "God has an anointing on you. I can see it. Come walk with me."

And with all these people waiting for him, with me beside him, we walked.

Two candidates I was running against looked concerned and were whispering. They didn't seem to like me talking to him, but Bishop Archer blew past them.

He goes, "Tell me, in thirty seconds or less, what is weighing on your mind."

"Sir," I said, "God called me to run for Congress. I'm as sure of that as I'm sure I'm talking to you now, and God never fails, but I'm afraid I might. This cross is heavier than I could tell you." Then everything poured out. "I'm being attacked. I'm being threatened. I'm being slandered. I'm being intentionally left out of everything. I'm being sabotaged. I spent thousands on signs, and they're all ruined. We have videos of people pulling up my signs. No one else's, just mine.

"All I want to do is save my kids' future. I was born in Texas, and I love my state and my country. I'm spending my own money while my own party spreads lies about me, when all I want to do is be part of the solution.

"I'm not Candace Owens. I don't have thirty million followers. How do I do what God wants me to do when I'm carrying the whole swamp on my back?"

"My dear," he said in his signature baritone voice, "God uses greatly those who are wounded deeply. Your betrayal is your blessing. God doesn't call the qualified, He qualifies who He calls. You are anointed."

"'Anointed?' I don't understand."

"Do you know how to tell the difference between real gold and fool's gold?"

"It's heat, the highest heat."

"That is correct. Gold is referenced more than any other metal in the Bible. Gold is valuable, like frankincense and myrrh. The highest heat burns away all its impurities until gold shines pure.

"God didn't put the fire there to burn you, Raven. He put it there to refine you."

I almost fell to my knees.

It was like his voice was flowing through me.

"God doesn't need you to have it all figured out. He just needs you to show up. Will you do what He calls you to do? God knows what He's doing. It was twelve years after David was anointed to be king before he actually ascended the throne."

His words fed my soul. The weight didn't go away, but I knew, *I knew*, I could bear it.

I felt inspired and ready to press on. I wanted Bishop Archer for my campaign, but he oversees fifty-three churches, is an author, speaker, and a celebrity, and I couldn't afford him.

Then God intervened once again. A few days after the gala, the bishop called me, and set my course on a new spiritual heading.

He said, "Whatever God is trying to do, He has told me to help and mentor you." My grandmother used to say, "God has the power to show you who is God."

That He did.

CHAPTER 10

GRASSROOTS

"Be not deceived, God is not mocked; for whatsoever
a man soweth; that shall he also reap."
—Galatians 6:7 (KJV)[1]

Grassroots organizations hold events, interact with voters, put out voter guides, and recommend candidates. They give the impression that they've thoroughly vetted the candidates, but that's not consistently what happens.

It's not surprising that political organizations are political. It's part of the coalition building necessary to reach voters and gain the momentum every successful campaign needs. The problem is those organizations represent their guides to voters as an objective vetting of candidates based on the values those movements espouse when they're not. Voting guides show up everywhere to include just outside the prohibited area at polling locations.

Voter influence is an ingrained process that we understand, even as kids when we're lined up picking teams for dodgeball. We pick players for our team based on who we like, how well we think they'll play, and what we think we know about them based on what we've seen and been told. That's voter influence. Every party does it. Any number of factors can influence a vote. It's subjective. It doesn't have to be fair, but when an organization specifically removes a lawful candidate from consideration or recommends a candidate because someone in that organization was paid off with cash or favors, when they say they've weighed the merits of every candidate, that's when it crosses the line into manipulation.

The response I got from one grassroots organization when I contacted them to say, "I was left off your candidate list, and it appears intentional," was such a telling exchange I'm including it below. I didn't pull my punches. I never do.

MY FIRST EMAIL:

From: Campaign
To: Grassroots Organization
RE: Your Voting Recommendations

I was completely and intentionally left off this. So, District Twenty-Six's only Texas-born, veteran-raised, minority, female, anti-abortion candidate able to speak credibly against CRT and race politics was excluded from your form. I was the second candidate to officially enter the race, which means you were able to find all the candidates running against me and exclude me. The fact that my name is not even listed, even if I had received no votes from your members prior to early voting in four days, is highly suspicious.

I would very much like to hear the perspective from your organization before I address what I believe to be collusion and misinformation intended to mislead Texas voters to support preapproved establishment candidates.

MY SECOND EMAIL:

From: Campaign
Date: February 10, 2022
To: Grassroots Organization
Subject: Raven Harrison was left off . . .

Good afternoon,

I just received your voter guide via email. At the very least, I'm extremely disappointed to see that my name was left completely off the listing for congressional district candidates for Texas Twenty-Six. I was the second candidate to officially announce, I have been listed on the secretary of state website since the very beginning, and I am on all official documents as a candidate. I do not believe this is a coincidence, but rather the latest in a string of similar "incidences" where I am being left off literature, vetting opportunities, ballots, and other items by those seeking to silence me, remove me from consideration, and mislead voters.

I have received no inquiries and no vetting from your organization. I have reached out to your organization several times over the past eight months trying to become involved with your group and allow them to vet and research me. I have signed up for the newsletter and participated in your various events.

I am the candidate for District Twenty-Six with the strongest military family background and the strongest candidate in the fight for the unborn, as the only candidate able to give birth. I am the strongest counterattack against the race politics the left is using to destroy our country, and you have left me off as the most viable option to move conservative values forward.

I would very much like to know if this "mistake" can be amended, or if you will be complicit in allowing the establishment to destroy our country. I await your prompt response.

THE RESPONSE:

On Feb 10, 2022, Grassroots Organization wrote:

It's not that you were left out. It's that we only list those candidates who received a vote. Apparently, no one on the leadership team in Denton County plans to cast a vote for you. **Maybe you haven't communicated your message, or maybe they're like me and get sick of people who list "minority" as if it's a credential.** I've copied the directors here in case they want to respond. Either way, our list is just a starting point for folks to do their own research, and that is clearly a race where there are no clear conclusions.

MY REPLY:

From: Campaign
Date: February 10, 2022
To: Grassroots Organization
Subject: Re: Voting Recommendations

The fact that I am a minority is not a credential I tout, it is a fact, and in my opinion, an asset to defeat the skewed narrative the radical left has deployed to destroy our country. I am absolutely disgusted with this narrative. As a minority woman raising mixed children dealing with bold-faced racism day in and day out, I find it wildly inappropriate and sickening that someone who supposedly represents the Republican Party has deemed it appropriate to insult my credibility. Race has nothing to do with my qualifications, but it does enhance my ability to shut down the idea that our party is predominately comprised of "old Caucasian men."

If you truly read my previous comment, you would have understood that I absolutely never requested special treatment. I simply asked for fair and equal treatment. The other candidates have never been purposely omitted from any voters guide regardless of their popularity or lack thereof. Our country is on the brink of disaster; as a true conservative, republican woman in this race who made the decision to put my life on hold and subject myself and my family to criticism and blatant racism by people like you only inspires me to fight harder for my country. I was inspired to run for Congress to defend the freedoms and liberties for all Americans, regardless of their color, creed, or gender. I fight this battle to end the corruption in our system that you now stand on and use as platform to instigate hatred and divide our party and country.

As I am not privy to the information that you claim to have received, which makes wild claims that "no one in Denton plans to cast a vote for me," I can only make assumptions about you and your character. These assertions look, sound, and feel an awful lot like collusion, as previously referenced in my initial communication with you. Please explain how there are four votes for an anonymous candidate, "under vote," with no name. My final deduction is that you listed nameless votes for a candidate with "no" votes but purposely omitted my name because you've deemed me "unpopular."

Unlike other candidates, I have a growing and popular social media following, billboards, endorsements, and literature all over town. However, I am the only candidate who has been repeatedly, and intentionally, left off Denton County events under the guise of "not knowing I was running for office." Then you insinuate that my communication is apparently the problem . . .

I would appreciate your express attention to this matter and expect a reasonable and rational response, or further discussion will be initiated by my legal team with your superiors.

If you hate email trails or skipped down, here's the play-by-play summary:

ME: I'm a candidate. I'm not listed. It doesn't look right. Can we fix the "mistake"?

HER: No. We only list candidates who received a vote. Apparently, no one on the leadership team plans to vote for you. Maybe you haven't communicated your message, **or maybe they're like me and get sick of people who list "minority" as if it's a credential.**

ME: If you only list candidates who receive a vote, explain how there is one vote for an anonymous candidate called "under vote" who's not on the ballot, but is listed four separate times? More concerning, you just outed yourself as a racist. Race has nothing to do with my qualifications, but it does enhance my ability to shut down the idea that our party is predominately comprised of "old, racist white men."

This exchange happened on Thursday. I updated my social media to show I was heading to a grassroots meeting in the morning. I didn't call the media; we were in the middle of primaries, and I didn't want to give the Democrats or anyone gunning for Republicans fuel for their fire. I had moved on after our email exchange, but some in the organization hadn't. One of my favorite grassroots organizations meets at 8:00 a.m. every Friday. They invite candidates to come meet their members, talk about issues, and discuss why we're the best candidate for the job.

Despite the resistance, I met with voters in the community regularly, and my message that a country without borders is not a country was well received. No one who has entered our country illegally should be receiving taxpayer money or benefits. Especially since Biden's wide-open borders hit Texans first and hardest of all Americans.

I arrived at the meeting early with my campaign manager, Lauren. There's a social before they call the meeting to order and a gentleman next to me said, "I saw that voters guide email exchange. It was horrible. I can't believe they said that."

"You and me both. But that's how it goes. Best to press on." I stood to line up with the other candidates to speak, when a woman behind me shouted, "Maybe you should stop telling people you're a minority." Her name was Hannah.

"Because they can't tell by looking at me?" I said, turning. "Do you want to talk about this?" I said, closing the distance. "Or are you just here to drop snide comments?"

Hannah was a member of the grassroots organization I had just confronted. She had a slender build, and streaked shoulder-length blond hair. I was in heels, and she was taller than me. I saw a few phones out recording.

So I asked her again, "Can we talk about this?"

"Well, you know, you didn't get a vote, and you're just trying to make us look bad," Hannah said, flailing her arms, and her nails sliced my forearm.

"You just scratched me," I said holding up my wrist, showing blood on my arm. "I'm not making you guys look bad. You're doing a spectacular job of that yourself."

I didn't know the board members of that organization by sight, but obviously they were there. I had only sent my email to the organizer listed on the guide, but the woman who responded copied all twelve board members on her racist tirade.

Several members of the group surrounded me, trying to intimidate me.

It wasn't working.

"How do I get a vote if I'm not listed as an option to vote for?" I said. "How does that work?"

"Well, we have the right to vote for whoever we want."

"You absolutely do. But is that what you tell voters? You say you vet candidates but provide no criteria. Your guide says in the fine print that seven anonymous members vote on the candidates, so you actually just vote for whoever you like, then tell voters you vetted them?"

She didn't say another word.

Another woman with sandy brown hair and overdone makeup stepped in, and put her finger in my face, growling, "I came here to set you straight."

"Oh." I stepped beyond the range of her hand. "So, I did properly communicate my message then?" I asked sarcastically. "Since you knew I'd be here."

And with that she just lost her ever-loving mind. "That's not the point! We can vote for whoever we want."

"Then who is 'under vote'? He's listed in different districts. He's not even a candidate."

"He withdrew."

"You gave one vote each to four different, nameless candidates who withdrew?"

I was getting jostled. Another woman yelled, "You just want us to put your name there if you didn't get a vote?"

"Absolutely," I said. "Just like every other candidate you listed."

Lauren, who was shaking hands and handing out literature, noticed I was encircled by people shouting at me. It looked like an unfair schoolyard fight with me being surrounded by several hostile women who were desperately trying to spin the optics of their racist assault on me, and she jumped right in the middle of it.

"Look how smug everyone looks," Lauren said, pushing herself into the circle of board members surrounding me. "Six, seven, no, eight against one. What a bunch of bullies."

"I still like my odds," I said. I wasn't looking for a fight, but I definitely was not going to back down or allow these declared racists to lay a finger on me.

Lauren is attractive and has a presence and they stopped like she had hit pause. "Your boss is a racist, plain and simple, and now you're attacking Raven? Most of you liked Raven and what she stands for, before your boss told you not to." They were starting to look uncomfortable. "Did she tell you to attack Raven? Or did you guys come up with that all on your own?"

"They're here for damage control," I said. "But it isn't looking good. Now I'm surrounded and bleeding." I met Hannah's glare. "Not the sound bite you were looking for?"

I left with my head held high. I wasn't going to give them the satisfaction. Let them try to manipulate and stream that. They couldn't defend what they'd done.

It was a shame. That organization had done great things in the past and most people who belonged to it were good men and women. One day I hope to have a real conversation with them, but I wasn't going to lose sleep over it. I had another gig to get to.

═══════════

The next day I fired Mitch and hired a security detail to keep an eye on my family and staff, and accompany me to my remaining events.

Mitch didn't take it well. "Why are you firing me?"

"Seriously? You failed to accomplish anything you were hired to do." I went down the list of things he said he'd deliver when I hired him.

"You said you would run my campaign, but you didn't. I had to find a campaign manager after you said you'd take care of it and didn't. I still don't have a dedicated fundraiser. You haven't set up any meetings for me since Burgess. And I don't have the endorsement from Trump you promised."

"Raven, you need to give my efforts a little more time to pay off. We have a complicated strategy that—"

"Mitch, I just can't shake the feeling that everyone else knows more about my campaign than I do. Why do you think that is?"

Silence.

"I paid your last invoice. We're done."

I hired Lauren from a referral I got from church, because even without political experience, she's a great organizer. She hit the campaign trail hard doing anything and everything that needed to be done. I don't know whether it was because of her talent at getting things moving again or because she's pretty, but people started whispering, as quiet as drunks, "There's that Jezebel." I heard jealous women calling her a hooker and a whore. That's how nasty it got, but she was unflappable. She's comfortable with who she is and laughed it off as "hater-aid" and got results.

Us making campaign progress generated an uncomfortable amount of hate, but time was ticking down to the election. We dealt with the hate by focusing on the awesome response we got from voters and showing up to everything we could, despite being intentionally excluded. We pressed on, and no matter how dark it got, Lauren could find ways to make the worst parts of it fun.

Mitch was out; Lauren was in. Donations were tight, and we were scrambling.

It wasn't just the grassroots organizations anymore. There was a coordinated effort to shut me out, but I was still crashing events. Still hearing, "Oh, I didn't know you were running." Still saying, "Yet here I am." Not backing down until they let me in.

All the other candidates knew about events in advance. A few of them even seemed uncomfortable about what was happening to me. If the establishment and corrupt Republicans In Name Only (RINOs) could try to silence me, they could silence anyone while preaching to voters they were working for change.

That year, just days before the primaries, was the Lincoln Reagan dinner (which for conservatives is a big deal), and this time I not only had an invitation, but also a confirmed table.

They call it a dinner, but it's a black-tie gala and one of the biggest networking and fund-raising events, in every state, for the Republican Party. In 2022, the keynote speaker for our Lincoln Reagan Dinner was Dennis Prager, and it was being held at election ground zero, in Denton, Texas.

I was one of the first candidates to buy a table for the gala, and following the disestablishment playbook, they put my table as far back from the stage as possible. But I wasn't about to let anyone relegate me to the shadows. Our round table was full of VIPs in smart tuxedos and silk dresses, and sitting nearest to me were my husband, as well as Bishop Archer, television and radio host Wayne Allen Root (who was once the vice presidential nominee for the Libertarian party before rejoining the Republican Party and endorsing Donald Trump), and Cindy Parker, the director at large for the Nevada Republican Club.

My security detail was also there, and it had already paid for itself. After the incident at the grassroots organization, they had stopped people from tailing me and my family and turned them away. Sean and David were my event security that night. They were keeping a watchful eye from a distance because there are rules you need to follow when you bring private security. Both were licensed and bonded. David was ex-military, and Sean was former law enforcement. For the first time in days, I felt at ease.

Lauren collected me to go on the stage for a closing event with all the elected officials and candidates, and I enjoyed different conversations along the way. My points that the geography of the swamp had spread all the way to local politics and my thoughts on ways to secure election integrity seemed to be well received.

Returning from the stage I passed Hannah, who literally drew blood at our last encounter. She was near a table in the middle of the crowd with a gentleman who seemed to have watery blue eyes and a receding thatch of dark hair, wearing a pink blazer. The pink blazer at a black-tie affair stood out, but she also had two small children at her table. They were cute, but it was unusual to see kids at a gala, much less past bedtime, and it made their table hard to miss.

I smiled at the kids, they waved back, but as soon as I walked past Hannah and her pink-swaddled man, the whispering began. One of the ladies I was walking with told me the man in pink was her boyfriend, now husband, and the chief administrator for Denton County Precinct 1. There were interesting stories swirling around about him.

I didn't know him; I didn't care. Aside from her snide comments in passing, they wouldn't have even been noteworthy, until she pointed at me laughing, and her pastel-blazered escort marched from the room like a man with a mission.

I had already put it out of my mind when I ran into Bishop Archer. Even with the headliners at the Lincoln Reagan Dinner, people queued up to talk to him. He was engaged in an animated conversation with the outgoing county Republican chairman. I waited not to interrupt, but Bishop Archer waved me over.

She turned snidely. "What are you doing here?"

"He's here with me." I smiled. "You didn't know?"

She went pale.

"Bishop Archer is a guest, at my table."

I would pay big money for a screenshot of what her face looked like at that moment.

Bishop Archer didn't know she was badmouthing me and when he continued, "God has something special in store for Raven. You have a real superstar here in her."

She choked on it so hard, I thought I'd have to perform the Heimlich maneuver. The woman spreading lies about me within the party had to listen to someone she respected supporting my campaign.

I felt vindicated, like a little justice had been served.

State Representative Tan Parker, from up the road in Flower Mound, was a great emcee. He started the event with a message everyone at the gala knew to be true in their bones. "If we surrender Texas, we all know what's at stake. We will lose this country, and never get it back." He kept the event moving.

Dennis Prager was bringing the house down; my husband and Bishop Archer and I were finishing our food when pink blazer strutted by looking pleased with himself. He joined up with Hannah and her sleepy kids, then locked eyes with me and grinned.

. . . Okay?

Before I could turn around, conversations stopped in a quiet bubble around a bull of a Denton County police officer in full gear, who stopped walking at our table right in front of me.

The mood turned suddenly serious. Everyone in the vicinity was looking around, wondering what was going on, and whispering in speculation.

He turned around a chair at my table. Then sat, facing me.

Crossing his arms. Narrowing his eyes. Staring.

I thought, *Well, isn't this interesting*. Then noticed everyone had followed his stare to me.

I had no sooner asked, "Officer, can I help you with something?" when Sean appeared by my side. "We need to talk." The policeman watched us closely, and I couldn't agree with Sean more.

"So what exactly is going on?"

"Ma'am, I have never, in my years of law enforcement, seen something so inappropriate." Sean's voice was deep and carried into the murmuring crowd. "I was in position in the private security area behind the tables when the Denton County Chief Administrator met that policeman and told him, 'We have a troublemaker, and you need to,'—and I quote—'watch the black girl.'"

The officer watching me heard Sean. Everyone around us did. And for an instant, you could see frustration cross his eyes before he bottled it up again behind a wall of professionalism. I leaned forward and said, "I understand you have your orders."

He nodded, almost imperceptibly, and followed them.

They put him in a position where no one should have to be.

Both of us knew what was really going on.

It didn't matter that this guy's girlfriend actually assaulted me, unprovoked, and that's why I had security in the first place. Or the fact that they had just violated my civil rights in front of witnesses, to racially profile and target a minority woman they didn't like politically.

It didn't seem to matter that it directly followed her grassroots comrade publicly and enthusiastically, flaunting herself as a racist.

It didn't matter that in the heart of Texas, in the middle of an election, in the year 2022, her boyfriend abused his elected power and had just confirmed that racism was alive and well in the party.

This "black girl" was a candidate for Congress in his district, and it did not matter.

From that point on, you couldn't take my picture without seeing a policeman glaring at me. No other candidate had to deal with optics like that. No candidate should have had to.

No one should be treated like that. Ever.

I was floored that that's where we are with the party. Nothing like that had ever happened to me on the campaign trail, but it happened there, at our biggest event just three days before primaries. The vibrancy of the gala turned dusty gray, and it felt like I was in East Berlin again. Conversations had stopped. All the furtive, dirty looks and hard stares. The hushed conversations because I represented American freedom. If you squinted, everyone was dressed the same. Only no one was abjectly poor and powerless; to the contrary, everyone in that room was rich by comparison, with the power to change our government, people's lives, and the world.

I was hurt and I was angry because I had done nothing wrong.

So many dark feelings welled up inside me, but sitting beside me was my husband, a veteran, my love. And my friend, a bishop and man of God.

I had the trust and confidence of everyone at my table.

And beyond the glare around me, I had the support of many, many more.

The fine people around us, wearing better than their Sunday best, gradually returned to their deals and conversations while I was under the watchful stare of a Denton County police officer. He was ordered to "keep an eye on the black girl" by the chief administrator for Precinct 1, who later resigned, and was fined $37,500 by the Texas Ethics Commission for his involvement in a "sham" political committee and potential forgery. US Representative Michael Burgess—who called me "Missy" and told me, "This district is affluent, sophisticated, and educated. They'll never accept you," was on the stage giving the outgoing Republican Party chair—who called me "a Democrat plant"—a farewell gift for her great service to Denton County.

We can do better. We must do better.

CHAPTER 11

GEOGRAPHY OF THE SWAMP

"When they call the roll in the Senate, the senators do not
know whether to answer 'Present,' or 'Not guilty.'"
—Theodore Roosevelt[1]

I had forty-eight hours left before the primary election. Two full days of
places to go, people to see, and my story to tell. Years ago, I would have
said the swamp was DC. Our capitol. The corrupt-beltway politicians
were selling out their constituents to line their pockets that President
Eisenhower had warned us about when he said, "In the councils of
government, we must guard against the acquisition of unwarranted
influence, whether sought or unsought, by the military-industrial
complex."[2] But that "unwarranted influence" has spread far beyond the
military-industrial complex and into every facet of government like a
disease. The swamp infiltrates everything. It has its own geography and
immoral ecosystem.

Our country was founded on Judeo-Christian values. We came
from unique and humble origins. Our country wasn't founded by an
elite ruling class, but by pioneers who left England because they were
the outcasts of society. Our forefathers were disposable to the British,
but we had resources they wanted, and as the crown imposed greater
control and higher taxation, a war to end their oppression ensued.

Our founding fathers lived under tyranny, fought for what they
believed in, earned their freedom, and knew that tyranny would return.
This is true in both walks of my lineage: American and Native American.

It was a revolutionary war because they envisioned something for
America that didn't exist in 1787: a government not ruled by kings and

emperors, but by "we, the people," built on freedom and the importance of the individual.

Our founding fathers framed our constitution to protect us. They understood how precious hard-won freedom is; they knew that without establishing precautions, our own government could take our freedom away.

Today we have the exact opposite kind of leaders in power. We have an aristocracy of elites, elected by the meek, who are robbing the people who put them in office. Our executive, legislative, and judicial branches are mired down and polluted to the point that they're no longer functioning. The first task of Congress is to produce a budget and set spending levels and limits. When was the last time that happened, without last-minute continuing resolutions, reconciliations, or adding to our already staggering national debt? The last time the US had zero deficit was 1835. Since 1960, the federal government has been in deficit all but nine years. And the last time we had a balanced budget was in 2001, according to the treasury, and 1996, according to the Hill and other sources.[3] This highlights a grim reality that politicians are more focused on keeping their jobs rather than *doing* their jobs.

If we ran our personal budgets like Congress, we'd be bankrupt or in jail.

At a firefighter's pancake breakfast, I was asked what I thought about the Democrats taking away our guns, and I said, "Beto shows up to one of his events with armed security and a handful of police he lobbied to defund. I blasted him on social media. I said, 'Hey, Beto, is your private security carrying rock salt in their guns or live ammo? And are those the same taxpayer-funded police escorting you that you wanted to defund?'"

His brainwashed minions shouted at me, "At least it's not an AR-15!" Seriously? So we protect banks, jewelry stores, sporting events, and politicians with armed security as if their lives are more valuable than ours. Meanwhile, our children get a paper sign telling bad people not to do bad things. It is twisted and sick.

Lately, their go-to gun control argument is, "Who actually needs an AR-15?" When that conversation comes up—and it always does—I remind them of our real history, that when the second amendment was written, they hadn't just finished deer hunting season. They had just finished liberating a country. The right to bear arms is about preventing tyranny, not bagging your limit. But they don't know about bag limits either.

And that's the point where all hell usually breaks loose. When radicals can't defend their position with facts, they move the goal posts or resort to violence.

All the politicians on the left standing up saying, "They want our guns," all have people with guns protecting them: secret service, their own private details—and these people don't carry sling shots; they're carrying live ammo.

It's not about gun control. It's about people control. To the liberal left, guns are okay, if their people are the only ones who have them.

They say, "See all these shootings. If we take all the guns away, this will stop, and everyone will be safe." But everywhere that policy has been put in place, after the guns were confiscated, safety did not improve. Shootings still happened, but only criminals and the government had the means to protect themselves—not the law-abiding citizens. What can the government do after they have taken away the guns of law-abiding people? The answer is: anything it wants.

I arrived just in time to slide into a podcast. While they were playing the lead-in video, I was fiddling with my headphones. I caught my breath as we went live.

"You know," the host said, turning to me. "We're back with Raven Harrison. She's running for Congress in our district. Raven, what's one thing you would do to curb corruption in the capitol?"

"Well, Mike, term limits are a great place to start, and I would prioritize getting that amendment passed. Giving Supreme Court justices lifetime appointments when they're in their seventies and eighties and nineties is a recipe for disaster. My husband, Paul, is an airline pilot, and you can't fly for an airline anymore after you reach sixty-five. You can still fly as a private pilot, but the FAA considers the risk too great for pilots flying passengers for an airline after reaching sixty-five. It's about safety and legitimate concerns about health and decision-making as we get older.

"So our government is clear that a highly trained and experienced pilot shouldn't be responsible for the safety of hundreds of people and their aircraft after age sixty-five, but the same government has nothing to say about a chief justice or congressman or president making policy decisions that affect over 300 million-plus people after sixty-five? Even for politicians I like and respect. Regular fresh ideas from individuals with experience outside the beltway is how we curb corruption from coming into government. Pumping fresh water into the swamp will ultimately flush the corruption out, even in less time if we drain the current residue. Congress should be a patriotic duty, not a final destination or elite-jobs program. We already have a two-term limit for the president. If it's good enough for the boss, why isn't it good enough for judges, the Senate, and Congress? America needs real leadership, making real decisions for the good of their constituents and our country. We can't continue to have people like Pelosi—in Congress since before the Internet—holding the United States in a death grip to consolidate her power and wealth at the expense of the people. That's the definition of corruption. But we can stop it.

"I'm slogging through the swamp right now, and it's exhausting. It's ankle-deep in free Texas, but if I stop moving, I'll sink; if we can't right this wrong, it will fall on our children.

"People don't think of the swamp as being at the local level. Even here, where concerned parents are now running for school boards. Nobody really cared about who was on the school board fifteen years ago, until they started pumping critical race theory (CRT) into the classroom along with sex education curriculums that promote high-risk sexual activities and seek to normalize those activities among children. Other curriculum topics have included disturbing and inappropriate images, gender studies, and links on how to find abortion clinics as well as instructions for children on how to hide their browser history from their parents.

"Who started pumping that garbage into the schools? The government did. But the government wasn't created to teach my kids morally bankrupt activism, and how to hide from me what they are teaching my kids. The government wasn't created to be a welfare state that pays people not to work and incentivizes the destruction of the nuclear family. Our families.

"How did we get here? First, take a hard look at education. From elementary school through high school all the way through college, liberalism has distorted education and created degrees that encourages inordinate debt to pursue work in fields with little chance of making a living and no chance of paying off their student loans. Yet somehow, it's someone else's fault those graduates aren't prepared to enter the workforce. Worse still, there's the arrogance that, rather than being accountable for loans contracts they took out—for degrees they chose— other hard-working Americans, many who never attended college, should shoulder their student loan debt so they don't have to pay for their degrees. It's ridiculous. If you or I take out a loan, that's on us. We're expected to pay it back. This isn't loan forgiveness. It is responsibility transfer. This is you paying off someone else's debt so the Democrats can buy their votes.

"Decisions and actions have consequences. We need teachers, not activists, in the classroom. We need educators, not social justice warriors who rewrite history and push depravity in shadow curriculums they keep hidden from parents. We need our children to learn to read and write, understand mathematics and history, and have the skills they need to be successful in life. They're supposed to teach them how to think, not *what* to think. But that's not what's happening anymore. All eyes are on Washington, but there's swamp, right here, we need to drain for our kids. For their future." A foremost responsibility is to hand over to the next generation an America as good or better than the one handed to us. If we don't fix this mess, how will they?

―――――

It was dark, and happy hour, when I arrived at the VFW hall. As a military brat, I always feel at home around vets. I love listening to their stories, many of which I have lived through. I've heard vets talk about miraculous and amazing and horrific things. Most of them are proud; some of them put their pride on the line to tell me what they'd been through. They told me about war. Some showed me their scars. A few talked about scars they had that no one could see. I wanted to know how they were treated when they came home. The bad was bad, but more recently, there was a lot of good and appreciation for their service in the community, but we still need to do more.

"Our military has been ravaged by radical ideology, inept leadership, and medical tyranny. As our enemies get stronger, our dedicated soldiers are overwhelmed by political correctness at their bases.

"The Biden administration forced an experimental 'vaccine' on our healthiest, finest-trained servicemen and women. Those who didn't take it were put out of the military as our nation struggles to recruit the soldiers, sailors, marines, and airmen we need in uniform. I will not turn a blind eye to the egregious abuses, disrespect, and mistreatment of our heroes in uniform.

"Congress must stand up and protect the men and women who risk their lives for this country. The damage the Biden regime has done to our military and veterans will take years to repair.

"We must return to the Reagan-era doctrine of peace through strength. I am working to rebuild our military and eliminate forced medical procedures. I am working to rebuild the shattered relationships with our allies, especially Israel, and our constituents. There must be accountability for those responsible for the lives and trust lost in Afghanistan. Some of you served there. Some of you lost friends there. Biden's withdrawal from Afghanistan was inept, his generals were mute, and terrorists already occupy their old strongholds—only now they're better equipped than they have ever been, with the weapons Biden left them. America always has, and must once again, lead the way to securing world peace."

I stayed longer, listening to their stories.

═══════

It was Monday morning. The day before the election. Paul made me tea, and I was on the road with Lauren before sunrise. After the Lincoln Reagan dinner, my media interviews were mostly podcasts going into election day.

A free press is crucial to the success of a democracy. The more objective, the better. The days of Walter Cronkite clearly and calmly discussing the happenings of the world on *CBS Evening News* are long gone. His program was one of the most-watched shows on TV, and he was widely regarded as "the most trusted man in in America." His approach to the news could be summed up by the catchphrase he used before signing off: "And that's the way it is."

Now ubiquitous media keeps the swamp fed and moist.

Historically, governments (in the form of propaganda) and media company owners sowing dissent have subverted the news for profit.

What was "yellow journalism" (designed to discredit competitors and create drama to fuel magazine and newspaper sales), has become big tech and media conglomerates fanning the flames of hate to create frenzied environments for clicks, likes, and advertising dollars . . . all while furthering their influence and socializing subversive agendas.

Lauren and I arrived at the community center of a large retirement community for brunch with the residents to talk about issues impacting Texas and discuss the concerns of our retirees. They were worried that social security was not keeping pace with the recent spikes in inflation, so I expected to talk about the economy. What surprised me was my first question.

"Hi, Raven. Thanks for coming all the way here. What do you think about politicians in Washington wanting to raise or lower the voting age?"

"I've heard arguments for and against both. You're an adult at eighteen years old. You're old enough to die in combat. If you're old enough to legally make your own decisions, and be held responsible for them, then you should be treated like an adult and be able to vote for the kind of country you want to live in.

"Now some folks argue that, at eighteen, young men and women really aren't mature enough to be adults, so the voting age should be higher. I think that's crazy. How many people in this room were working before they were eighteen, or in the service fighting a war, or starting families? You were old enough to do all that, but not old enough to vote according to your values for what you believe in? That's absurd.

"And then there are the progressive liberals who want to lower the voting age, so malleable children can vote, just like they want five-year-olds to change their gender. Ironically, Burgess was the only 'Republican' to vote with Pelosi and her merry band of communists to attempt to lower the voting age to sixteen. It's ludicrous. They are children, something an OB-GYN doctor like Burgess should know, and children lack the maturity and experience to make life-changing decisions. That's why parents raise them until they're adults who can take care of themselves. Legally, that happens at eighteen.

"A lot of people are snug and comfortable with the wool pulled over their eyes. I'm not one of them. I say we focus on real problems and not waste time arguing about made up things like letting children vote.

"One very real problem we have right now is the economy, particularly inflation. Everything is more expensive: we pay more for less food, mortgage rates are going up, fuel price hikes are making the cost of utilities, products, and services spike across the country. Everything is now more expensive for everyone.

"Inflation is the highest it's been since the 1970s when we had double-digit inflation, and many of you remember gas rationing and how hard inflation made it to stretch a dollar. We must fight for Texas and be a voice for everyone in America.

"Just two short years ago, under Trump, we had a thriving economy. But not anymore. The Trump-era tax cuts fueled historically low unemployment and historic stock market gains, particularly among minorities. Manufacturing jobs returned to the United States, and our communities and low gasoline prices were the crown jewel of the United States' newfound energy independence. The Biden administration has cast away that independence to pander to special-interest groups. We have record inflation and an anemic economy that is on life support.

"I vehemently oppose government overreach, mandates, and crisis-driven spending. I am working to end uncontrolled, unsustainable, and wasteful spending. I will stand up for small businesses and prioritize rebuilding them after the destruction caused by draconian COVID-19 policies."

I stayed longer than I had intended. There was a lot to discuss, but I still had three stops left to make.

I was taught actual civics in school, and we learned about communism as part of our lessons in actual history. It's obvious the youth of today have not. I've also read *The Communist Manifesto*, Stalin's doctrines, almost everything by Karl Marx, and Hitler's *Mein Kampf*. I read to know my enemy's playbook, so I can recognize my enemy and engage them. I also lived in Communist Germany. Sometimes our enemies are hiding in plain sight: young American socialists indoctrinated by academia, the Marxist founders of BLM, the media and government's exploitation of communist doctrines and tactics to centralize control.

How do they push a country toward communism?

They have a precedent; Stalin, Marx, and Hitler all left playbooks on how to do it. First, you make people afraid. You break up their support structures like family and religion so they're reliant on the government.

You divide citizens into groups, and you set them against each other. You tell people that it's not their fault, and someone else is to blame for their lack of success or misfortune. Finally, you give them a solution that only party elites in the government can execute. That's where we are today.

It can be summed up in one word: pacification.

Increasingly, young people aren't learning how the government works in civics; their opinions are formed by social media. We once used truth as a part of critical thinking to navigate deception and lies, but those hard truths are being replaced by "personal truths" based on limited experience, idealism, and situational morality.

I don't often get to talk to college-aged students. Many campuses actively oppose ideas different from their worldview and respond violently to conservative speakers looking to open an honest dialogue. Not long ago, university professors routinely taught their students to question everything. In 2022, many undergraduate programs incentivize what a student *should* think at the expense of how *to* think by applying logic and their own critical-thinking skills.

I was at a coffee shop talking to a conservative group with a cross section of students. The ones who weren't going to listen to anything I had to say left, but a good-sized group remained; it was all women, and we had a frank conversation.

The first question was, "What do you say when you are constantly told that there are over fifty genders, and then someone says, 'I decided yesterday I'm a woman, and now I'm going to change with you and use the same bathroom?'"

"I say, you need to check your school's policies, let them know you're uncomfortable, and make them accommodate you and the other girls' needs as well. There are legal ways to address it if they won't, and there are organizations who can help you with that. Call your local representative right away.

"I don't mince words. As a woman, I am complicated, but made in God's image. Growing your hair out and putting on makeup and dresses does not make you a woman. Live your life how you want. As for me, saying you identify is no different than saying you pretend to be. That doesn't mean that you don't have the freedom to live and think as you please. It means that we don't change science and facts to accommodate feelings. Live your best life.

"I told my kids to ask their teachers, if it came up, how can you feel like something you're not genetically wired to be? This is not a social experiment. How can I say I feel like a gecko if I'm not cold-blooded and I don't hit that chromosomal makeup? I can empathize with what I think it feels like, but I don't actually know how it feels to be a cold-blooded reptile. Period.

"It used to be when science and facts did not support the argument, people would abandon the arguments; now when the science and facts don't support the arguments, people abandon the science.

"Biological men will never have periods; they will never give birth and will never breastfeed. They also naturally produce more testosterone and muscle mass than I have as a woman. Those are biological and scientific facts. They can be ignored but not changed by woke feelings.

"I was a tomboy; I wasn't a boy. I was a tomboy. A rugged, non-dress wearing, falling-out-of-trees, girl. And I'm so glad no one came around pushing pills and procedures when I was in the chaos of puberty, telling me I was really a boy and to take these pills to shrink my boobs and make it so I can never have kids and never have to worry about PMS or a period ever again. They say, 'Now you can live as who you really are.'

"No, I'm a tomboy, not a boy. I worked it out. And if you're gay, you're gay, and that's your business. I think we have to acknowledge that growing up and puberty is hard on all kids. But permanently altering their bodies because they show an interest in something else for a moment or go through a phase and then expect a child to make those kinds of life-altering decisions should be a crime, but it's happening every day, and it must stop.

"People can decide to be whoever they want to be when they're adults. I was a pretty smart kid, but I can't even imagine making a decision like that at eight or twelve. I literally woke up one day in college and decided, you know what? I think today I want to look like a girl and wear a dress today. It was that profound.

"Today, educators and activists would try to take that away from me because it was in my best interests and for my own good. But it's not. A child's body isn't mature, and the brain is still developing into your twenties.

"Puberty blockers and gender reassignment treatment and surgery for minors isn't about tolerance or freedom or choice. It's about the sterilization of children and grooming."

I was tired and satisfied when I pulled into my driveway. I had talked at every forum and with every voter who would hear me. My message had touched thousands of people. I had spirited debates, parking lot arguments, and great conversations with people who shared the same concerns I did. They felt betrayed by the elected officials dismantling the America they loved. Everyone wanted a stronger, safer Texas. Schools that taught their kids what they said they would. A good life for themselves and their families. They wanted leaders who reflected their beliefs and values. I wanted to give them the America they deserved. A native-born Texan fighting for Texas values and freedom.

I said everything I had to say.

CHAPTER 12

ELECTION DAY

"I do solemnly swear (or affirm) that I will support and defend the Constitution of the United States against all enemies, foreign and domestic; that I will bear true faith and allegiance to the same; that I take this obligation freely, without any mental reservation or purpose of evasion; and that I will well and faithfully discharge the duties of the office on which I am about to enter: So help me God."
—The Oath of Office[1]

The oath for Congress is the same oath my parents swore as Air Force officers. There's a poetic justice to that. They took their oath to "support and defend the Constitution of the United States against all enemies, foreign and domestic" seriously. They lived it. I believe in it, and regardless of the path I take, I will follow in their footsteps and take up the mantle to fight for and protect our country.

America has been betrayed by the same people who have benefited most from her freedom and gifts. I will keep fighting to get our constitutional freedoms back.

It was election day. I'd been campaigning at every event I could get into, taking care of my kids, and my husband was still flying.

I could feel the exhaustion setting in. I would have preferred to stay home and just relax with my family. After all the lying, cheating, and deception, I didn't need a crystal ball to know the results, but my team needed the resolution and a chance to decompress. So we took it.

It was Bishop Archer's last night in town, and we all met at his hotel suite for the viewing party. Paul brought the kids over when he got back, and the party grew. Patriots who supported me during the campaign joined in.

It took a while for the results to come in. It would be a late night for the kids, so we set them up in a room to watch shows.

The mood shifted from relaxed to somber. The early votes were in. Even after the last two weeks of grinding, I was dead last.

I didn't feel like the results were the true measure of what I could do, how I performed, and how hard the campaign team had worked. I felt like this was a measure of how good the swamp was at keeping people out, and it wasn't just me. We had friends in other districts who were running, men and women who experienced the same pushback we did, and I wasn't the only one prevented from fundraising. It was widespread through several districts, and if you can't fundraise, you can't broadcast your message out.

It was unsettling to know it was a bigger problem than just me. We all had stories, but there was a common thread: if the establishment didn't want you to run, they did everything they could to mute your message and freeze you out. This was Republicans squelching Republicans, not mentoring or growing talent in the party. Just holding on to power as tight as they could.

There were no tears. There was no crying. We had everyone there. The reports came in, and the results were indicative of how hard we had to work to make any headway.

Not a surprise, but disappointing for Patience and Major to see Mommy losing. It was a teachable moment.

I felt disappointed the voters did not know what had happened.

I took pride in the fact that I managed to get the number of votes I did with everything stacked against me.

I did better on election day than I did in early voting, when the party organizations had their guides out and volunteers were telling people not to vote for me. At one polling location, Lauren and I came across a young man who told an undecided voter not to vote for me.

"Hey, why is that?" I asked.

"We were told to only push the candidates listed in the guide."

So I introduced myself. "I'm Raven Harrison," and his jaw dropped. "I'm the only candidate who has military parents, and I'm the only candidate born in Texas." We talked a bit.

"I'm so sorry," he said. "Now I feel really guilty about doing this."

"It's okay. You didn't know what they were doing. Thank you for giving me the benefit of the doubt, and letting me tell you who I am. I appreciate it."

"I'm glad we got to talk. I won't be doing this next year."

It's a hard truth to learn that not everyone who smiles is your friend. Not liking me is your prerogative, but lying to people about me is manipulation. It's no different than what the Democrats are doing. They're just out in the open about it.

What I really remember from election night wasn't the disappointment that we lost; it was the sense of pride in how far we'd come and what we accomplished.

Some say I came in last. I say we came in first, for carrying the entire establishment swamp on our back.

I did it without all the fundraising. I did it with no party support. I did it with the highest-ranking official in the Denton County Republican Party spreading lies about me.

Then the first round of phone calls came in from everywhere. High-profile people at the highest level offering their support and encouragement, saying, "Raven, we didn't find out about you until too late. We can't wait for the next one. We are on Team Raven. You know we'll be ready next time."

I'm fighting for my children and my family, and that is bigger than a title. I won't forget how being starved feels. God willing, my children will never know how that feels.

I'm even fighting for the woman who scratched me. And the guys who had the police harass me because of my skin color.

And I'm fighting for the ones who left me off the voters guide ballot because they don't know what they are ushering in. All these corrupt people have ever known is freedom. They won't last a minute if communism takes hold. Right now, people are choosing not to fight back; in the communist utopia, they won't be able to.

The bishop taught me how to tap into God, into my faith, and it has changed my life.

I've grown. I'm walking my intended path. I'm different now than I was when I started this campaign. What would have been a Race2theRaven for Paul's birthday was a run for Congress, and it was some race.

My mother often told me that there is true evil in the world, and once, I had to change my name because of that evil. Patriots, including my parents and husband, fought for the rights and freedom we have today. I saw someone die for freedom once. When you've seen that, it changes you. You understand what we have. You realize why people are so desperate to come to the United States.

I'm still in physical therapy because a woman hit me with her car after the election screaming, "I know who you are," and other hateful things about me and what I stand for.

My legs still hurt, but I walk a little farther every day, and I won't be stopped.

I've passed through pain and fire, but every ache and burn taught me something I needed later. My journey gave me a toughness to persevere. How many times have I wanted to say, "No more, make it stop. Why, Lord, why?" But I didn't stop. I kept moving forward. I have faith. I'm marching to God's plan. He forges keys in us to open doors we cannot see from where we are standing now, but as we climb higher, those keys will open locks in doors that can't be broken down.

I know who I am. Looking back, I've come a long way.

Today, I not only fight for Texas, but also for the whole of the conservative movement. The doors God opens, no man can close. The voice they tried to silence has now been amplified to a magnitude that cannot be ignored. I have a podcast, (*Raven's Radar*), this book, and a robust social media following of patriots I wouldn't trade for anything. The truth is coming out, and patriots are standing with me to return America to all its glory. I am no longer a spectator grateful for the sacrifices of those before me. I am now a de facto general on the front lines of the conservative movement fighting for freedom. War isn't won by politicians; it's won by soldiers. I am now the Conservative Warrior and a fire-breathing force for God. As the evil works overtime trying to anticipate my next move—Will she run again? What will she run for? What is her next move?—I stay the course. They can mock me, insult me, and conspire against me, but they cannot stop me. I am Raven. The Conservative Warrior. Called by God. Raised by patriots.

Deterred by nothing.

The Devil whispers, "You cannot withstand the storm." The Conservative Warrior replies, "I am the storm."

EPILOGUE

For her entire life, my mother had been fiercely protective of her privacy. Always. She wouldn't even tell me how old she was. My dad was just the opposite; he wore it like a badge of honor. I started noticing troubling signs of her decline and, in July 2014, three days after having surgery, my worst fears were confirmed. She was diagnosed with Alzheimer's and dementia and was given three-to-nine years to live.

Devastating would be the understatement of the century. The woman who loved and protected me and sacrificed so much will soon be unaware I even exist. It is truly the long, excruciating goodbye. I speak of her often, but I do not provide details on her condition out of respect. I just make sure she knows how much I love her. I hope she lives long enough to see me take an oath of office to defend the country she gave so much for.

My mother used to always tell me that God is the only constant in life, your only port in the storm. You'll be basking in the sun one moment and getting smashed against the rocks the next. Whether you are riding the wave or getting crushed beneath it is up to you.

She was betrayed in one way or another by almost everyone she trusted; she grew to trust no one. Even with my dad, she never fully let her guard down. She had to fight for everything she had, and nothing came easy.

As a girl, she had to be escorted by the police to school just after segregation was abolished. They refused to grade her papers in college due to her being the first and only female and woman of color in the engineering program.

There were times when I was a girl when some in the military refused to salute her.

I only ever saw her fight. The last time I spoke with her she said, "The world is waiting for you to fail; the best revenge is to succeed, and failure is not an option."

My father taught me to shoot before I could drive, and I was required to learn the language of wherever we lived, no matter how brief.

He told me, "Jesus wasn't betrayed by the masses, but rather those closest to him. Be mindful of who you let in your inner circle. Brutus had to be close enough to harm Caesar."

It turned out to be prophetic. At least regarding the election.

I'm still getting attacked and threatened and lied to and about.

I'm still trying to get people who hate me on board to help me save this country.

This is not about me. This is way bigger than me. The primaries were dirty politics and horrible and worse than I could have imagined.

Racism is a factor, but the problem in District Twenty-Six isn't racism. I grew up here with real Texans. We played together, worshiped together, laughed, and cried together. We had each other's backs. They couldn't care less what color I am, and I them. They just want to protect Texan values.

The problem is deep-seated corruption. It's about money. The swamp doesn't want it to change because it's lucrative. It wasn't Democrats that tried to sabotage me. Not leftists or liberals. It was my fellow Republicans and precinct chairs and county commissioners.

They had me racially profiled, and it divided the party. I felt trapped.

I felt like there was no course for justice, and that made me angry.

I was at the Lincoln Reagan dinner on my husband's arm, dressed to the nines at an event important people had invested a lot to attend, when a woman who assaulted me misused the police to harass and vilify me. It was pure, unadulterated swamp. Racial division, political injustice, and corruption were exemplified in that moment to manipulate an election. After the primaries, I learned that every single one of the other candidates had paid her boyfriend to be in that voter guide. Nothing surprises me anymore.

So how do I fix this?

I can't be a Democrat. Democrats founded the KKK and the Democrats fought *for* slavery and segregation, and even today, the apple doesn't fall far from the tree.

After everything that's happened, many people have advised me to file as an independent and run again to challenge Burgess, and I have all the justification in the world to do it. But I know who I am.

I'm a conservative constitutional, America-first Republican, and I choose to adhere to the principles on which the Republican party was founded, regardless of how many in our party have abandoned them. I choose to rise above the dirty politics, and I choose to fight with everything I have to hand my children the free America I was given.

I choose to be the change I wish to see.

ACKNOWLEDGMENTS

I would like to thank my parents, Lieutenant Colonel Mae Friel and Lieutenant Colonel John Zebelean III USAF (retired), for their love, bravery, sacrifices, and dedication—the very reasons I have such an incredible story to share. They are true warriors and patriots who taught me gratitude, humility, and perseverance. They gave me a Christian foundation—the light that has guided me through the darkest chapters of my life. It is because of them that I am a survivor, not a victim. I am proud to carry the warrior spirit of my Native American heritage into the next chapter. My mother is a pioneer who took off into the wind her entire life. My father is a decorated war hero, bold and charismatic, who stood unapologetically against racism and scorn to raise me as proof that your choices—not your circumstances—define your greatness.

A popular saying states, "When the student is ready, the teacher will appear." By the grace of God, during one of the most difficult sections of my journey to God's purpose, Bishop Ronaldo Archer came into my life as a mentor. Many people can change your mind, but few can change your life. He has taught me so much. I have a relationship with God that I never dreamed was possible. The pain and struggles of my youth have become the very source of my strength in maturity. "God uses greatly those who have been wounded very deeply. Little becomes much in the Hands of the Lord." I've learned to turn my pain into power, and I live in the faithfulness of God's word.

I would like to thank President Donald J. Trump for inspiring the political course I currently walk. My daughter's belief in you and defense of what you stand for has changed our lives. I intend to demonstrate that same courage and loyalty in supporting the greatest president of my time. Thank you, sir. This Conservative Warrior is ready to stand with you for the Biblical battle for our freedom.

I would like to thank Commissioner of the Texas Department of Agriculture, Sid Miller, who is a servant of the people, a man of God, and holds the principles of a true gentleman. Thank you, sir, for judging me by the content of my character and not the color of my skin. You exemplify the very heart of the Texas I was born to. You love Texas and America as much as I do, and I'm honored to work with you and Deb in this modern-day version of cowboys and Indians.

I would like to thank Todd Smith, an incredible strategist, veteran, and friend. Your loyalty is second to none, and I am blessed to call you family.

I would like to thank my publisher, Brown Books, for helping me through this process to get my message out there and show people what it means to be a true warrior fighting for our country. I would like to specifically thank Tom Reale for guiding me through the process, Bill Riley for both his military service and his hard work in bringing my story to light, and Danny Whitworth for the patriotic portrayal of my heritage and American ideals on the cover.

I would like to express my gratitude and love to my second parents in heaven, Mildred Georgette and Howard Lee Harrison, who loved and accepted me from the moment we met. You trusted me with what you cherished most in the world. You gave me a name and a legacy I could be proud of, and I will keep my promise to work to ensure that Patience grows up to be the lady and Major the gentleman that their grandparents were. I miss you.

I would like to acknowledge and celebrate my amazing husband, USAF (ret.) Major Paul Harrison—my rock, my inspiration, and the love of my life. You are generous, humble, kind, and attentive; you make me feel like the luckiest woman alive. You catch me when I fall, encourage me when I struggle, and celebrate me when I succeed. After a lifetime of chaos, you have given me the thing that had always eluded me: a safe port in the storm . . . a home. You remind me that planes take off into the wind. I am honored to be your wife, and I will work every day to be worthy to carry the baton to fight for our country as you did in your military career. I am your forever copilot. I love you beyond words and without limits.

Thank you to Jeff Crilley, Real News and my Fox News Radio family, the patriots in District Twenty-Six, and conservatives around the world who have joined me in this fight.

NOTES

CHAPTER 1: ACCIDENTS

1. Ronald Reagan, "January 5, 1967: Inaugural Address (Public Ceremony)," Ronald Regan: Presidential Library & Museum, National Archives, January 5, 1967. https://www.reaganlibrary.gov/archives/speech/january-5-1967-inaugural-address-public-ceremony#:~:text=Freedom%20is%20a%20fragile%20thing,only%20once%20to%20a%20people.
2. "The Declaration of Independence," America's Founding Documents, National Archives, last updated September 20, 2022. https://www.archives.gov/founding-docs/declaration.
3. Abraham Lincoln, *Abraham Lincoln papers: Series 3. General Correspondence*. 1837–1897: Abraham Lincoln, [November 1863] (Gettysburg Address: Nicolay Copy), November 19, 1863, Manuscript/Mixed Material. https://www.loc.gov/item/mal4356500/

CHAPTER 2: DOGS WITHOUT WHISTLES

1. Langston Hughes, "Dreams," *The Collected Poems of Langston Hughes* (New York: Alfred A. Knopf/Vintage, 1994).

CHAPTER 3: WAKE-UP CALL

1. Martin Luther King, Jr., *Strength to Love* (Cleveland, Ohio: Collins + World, 1977).

CHAPTER 5: CALL . . . OR CALLING

1. Thomas S. Monson, "U of U Commencement Remarks From President Thomas S. Monson," May 12, 2007, University of Utah, Ogden, Utah, UNews Archive, last updated March 25, 2011. https://archive.unews.utah.edu/news_releases/u-of-u-commencement-remarks-from-president-thomas-s-monson/

2. Daniel Hornstein, "A Spectre is Haunting . . . Mainstream Conservativism: Anti-Communism and the Construction of 'Radical-Left Democrats,'" McGill University, Montreal, June 2021. https://escholarship.mcgill.ca/concern/theses/rx913v62c.
3. "Fascism," Merriam-Webster, accessed February 17, 2023. https://www.merriam-webster.com/dictionary/fascism

CHAPTER 6: TEXAS

1. Liz Curtis Higgs, "Pray Like Everything Depends on God," Devotions, Proverbs 31 Ministries, October 13, 2014. https://proverbs31.org/read/devotions/full-post/2014/10/31/pray-like-everything-depends-on-god

CHAPTER 7: CAMPAIGN TRAIL

1. J.R.R.Tolkien, *The Fellowship of the Ring* (London, England: Harper Collins, 1991), 264.

CHAPTER 9: MENTOR

1. Newt Gingrich, Amy D. Berstein, Peter W. Bernstein, *Quotations from Speaker Newt: The Little Red, White and Blue Book of the Republican Revolution* (New York City, New York: Workman Publishing Co, 1995).

CHAPTER 10: GRASSROOTS

1. Gal 6:7 (King James Version)

CHAPTER 11: GEOGRAPHY OF THE SWAMP

1. "Sermon Quotes on Politics," The Pastor's Workshop, accessed February 17, 2023. https://thepastorsworkshop.com/sermon-quotes-on-politics/
2. "President Dwight D. Eisenhower's Farewell Address (1961)," Milestone Documents, National Archives, last updated December 15, 2022. https://www.archives.gov/milestone-documents/president-dwight-d-eisenhowers-farewell-address

3. Bill Fay, "Timeline of the US Federal Debt Since Independence Day 1776," Debt.org, last updated October 12, 2021. https://www.debt.org/faqs/united-states-federal-debt-timeline/#:~:text=However%2C%20President%20Andrew%20Jackson%20shrank,country%20was%20free%20of%20debt; "Larger Federal Deficits & Higher Interest Rates Point to the Need for Urgent Action," US Government Accountability Office, May 5, 2022. https://www.gao.gov/blog/larger-federal-deficits-higher-interests-rates-point-need-urgent-action#:~:text=However%2C%20this%20pattern%20has%20changed,if%20no%20action%20is%20taken.; "Policy Basics: Deficits, Debt, and Interest," Center on Budget and Policy Priorities, last updated July 29, 2022. https://www.cbpp.org/research/federal-budget/deficits-debt-and-interest.

CHAPTER 12: ELECTION DAY

1. "Oath of Office," United States Senate, accessed February 17, 2023. https://www.senate.gov/artandhistory/history/common/briefing/Oath_Office.htm#:~:text=I%20do%20solemnly%20swear%20(or,that%20I%20will%20well%20and.

EPILOGUE

1. David Archambault II, "Taking A Stand at Standing Rock," The New York Times, August 24, 2016. https://www.nytimes.com/2016/08/25/opinion/taking-a-stand-at-standing-rock.html

ABOUT THE AUTHOR

=========

Raven Harrison, known as the Conservative Warrior, is a Texas-born, former congressional candidate, author, political strategist, activist, business owner, wife of a retired USAF C-17 pilot, mother of two, and the daughter of two retired United States Air Force lieutenant colonels. Raven is married to United States Air Force C-17 pilot, Major Paul Harrison (retired). They live and attend church just north of Dallas, Texas. They have two children, Patience and Major.

Raven grew up an only child in a military-family dynamic that saw both her mother and father absent up to 325 days in any given year, engaged in high-powered, dangerous, and classified missions from the Pentagon. Her parent's path as defenders of this nation had Raven living in some of the most isolated, hostile, and dangerous war zones around the world. Academically gifted, Raven entered college at age sixteen and adjusted to the challenges of an environment in which she was two years younger than her peers. The euphoria of such an achievement was marred when Raven's life was threatened by terrorists attempting to access her parent's top-level security clearance by harming and/or ransoming her life. Despite being forced to change her name and invoke drastic security measures, Raven went on to excel in an executive career with premier global marketing agencies, responsible for accounts in the tens of millions for corporate giants such as IBM, Food Lion, and Shell Oil. Raven went on to create two successful marketing companies and was an industry pioneer.

Raven's life was forever changed when her then-eight-year-old daughter was almost expelled for voting for President Trump in a mock-election social experiment hosted by her elementary school. Raven was shocked and outraged; from that moment of betrayal, Raven was catapulted to the public eye as a firebrand general in the historic war for parents' rights against indoctrination in American schools. Raven was called by God to fight not only the betrayal of her children, but also the betrayal of America. Her lifetime in service to those in service to America led her to strike a blow to the evil that is enveloping our government. Raven and her family moved back to her native home of Texas, put aside her business interests, and stepped up to run for Texas's Twenty-Sixth Congressional District of the United States. Raven would soon learn that the corruption she sought to face was much deeper and widespread than she ever imagined, and had infiltrated almost every facet of her beloved Texas.

Raven's journey as constitutional conservative, military-bred, Native-American-and-African-descent woman wading through the corrupt and volatile world of modern day politics is nothing short of amazing. Combined with her incredible pedigree and personal experience present at such pivotal—and monumental—events like the Cold War, communism, the Vegas massacre, and 9/11 gives her a powerful and riveting firsthand perspective of the events that have shaped and divided modern history. *Raven's Mantle* is the made-for-TV story of Raven Harrison: her broken childhood, battles with extreme racism and terrorism, her triumph over unimaginable heart break, and her relationship with Christ as well as tribulations, adversity, and the unprecedented assault on freedom that has brought Raven to the front lines and created an unstoppable force. She is now a ferocious leader of the conservative movement, not only in Texas but also across the nation. It made Raven a voice for the heart of America; it made her the Conservative Warrior.

Raven homeschools her children while she fights on the front lines of the conservative movement. She speaks against government corruption at venues around the country while championing pro-life efforts, anti-CRT rhetoric, and other conservative causes. Raven is a contributor on Fox News Radio and has a weekly, celebrity-filled podcast, *Raven's Radar*.

The Devil whispers, "You cannot withstand the storm." The Conservative Warrior replies, "I am the storm."